Good Housekeeping's
MEAT and other MAIN DISHES

By the
Food Editors
of
Good
Housekeeping
Magazine

ILLUSTRATIONS BY
DAVID CUNNINGHAM

PHOTOGRAPHS BY
JAMES VILES

Contents

Published by
Consolidated Book Publishers
1727 South Indiana Avenue, Chicago, Illinois 60616

D1533795

Meat is still the all-time favorite main dish, and Americans are great meat-eaters. But lately we've noticed a trend away from the standard meat-and-potatoes meal.

Meat and other Main Dishes

Today the main dish is often likely to be adapted from an Oriental recipe, or borrowed from a Central European cuisine. In other words, it's likely to be *different!* So, in this book, you will find not only meat (and potato) recipes with a difference, but also an intriguing variety of other main-dish recipes—fish, shellfish, poultry, rice, and pasta dishes—to satisfy almost any flavor (and budget) requirements you may have.

Top-quality beef is bright red, well streaked (marbled) with thin veins of fat, and has a white, firm fat covering. In lower grades the red deepens, there is less marbling, and the fat takes on a yellowish cast. Many lower-grade cuts are every bit as flavorful as top-quality, but are likely to be less tender; so don't miss our tasty ways of braising, stewing, and even broiling such cuts.

OUR CHUCK STEAK WITH HORSE-RADISH SAUCE
(Pictured here)

1 chuck steak, 1½ inches thick, without bone (about 3 pounds)	Seasoned instant meat tenderizer Horse-Radish Sauce, below

About 1½ hours before serving:
1. Sprinkle each side of steak with 2 or 3 teaspoons tenderizer, then pierce both sides *very well* with fork. Let stand at room temperature 1 hour.
2. Preheat broiler 10 minutes, or as manufacturer directs. Place steak on broiler rack, then broil 10 minutes on each side, or until medium-rare.
3. Meanwhile, make Horse-Radish Sauce.
4. Serve steak, cut into 1-inch slices, with sauce, green beans with squash, crisp browned potatoes and green salad. Makes about 6 servings.

HORSE-RADISH SAUCE: In medium saucepan melt 3 tablespoons butter or margarine; stir in 3 tablespoons regular all-purpose flour. Then stir in 1 cup milk and 1 cup water; bring sauce to boil, stirring, then simmer 1 minute. Stir in 2 teaspoons horse-radish, 1½ teaspoons prepared mustard, ½ cup snipped parsley, and 1½ teaspoons seasoned salt. In small bowl beat 2 egg yolks with 6 tablespoons commercial sour cream; stir in some of sauce; pour back into saucepan; bring almost to boil.

CHUCK STEAK IN PAPILLOTE

1 4-pound chuck steak, 1½ inches thick, with bone Instant meat tenderizer	5 to 6 medium carrots 1 envelope onion-soup mix

About 2 hours and 15 minutes before serving:
1. Start heating oven to 300°F.

Our Chuck Steak with Horse-Radish Sauce

2. Treat steak with tenderizer as label directs.

3. Slice pared carrots ⅛ to ¼ inch thick.

4. Sprinkle some of soup mix in center of large piece of foil; lay steak on top of it; then sprinkle with rest of soup mix. Now place carrots on steak; wrap all well in foil. Place in shallow pan.

5. Bake 2 hours, or until fork-tender.

6. Transfer steak, still in foil, to serving platter; open up foil, fold back edges, exposing carrots and steak; skim off fat from surface of gravy. Nice served with broiled frozen French fries, succotash, and chocolate layer cake. Makes 4 or 5 servings.

FRED'S FLANK STEAK

1 2-pound flank steak	2 tablespoons soy sauce
2 teaspoons garlic-flavor monosodium glutamate	1 tablespoon sherry
	1 teaspoon liquid honey

At least 2 hours before serving:

1. Trim excess fat from steak; with sharp knife score, then sprinkle each side with half of monosodium glutamate. Lay steak in baking dish.

2. Combine soy sauce, sherry, and honey; brush one side of steak with half of this marinade; repeat on other side. Refrigerate at least 2 hours, turning about once an hour.

3. When ready to broil, preheat broiler 10 minutes, or as manufacturer directs. Brush steak with remaining marinade.

4. Broil 3 to 4 minutes on each side. Then slice thin, at an angle, across grain. Makes 6 to 8 servings.

STEAK FEAST

1½ cups bottled teriyaki barbecue marinade	½ teaspoon ginger
	Butter or margarine
1 chuck steak, 3½ inches thick (about 8 pounds)	2 16-ounce cans tiny whole beets
Seasoned salt	2 10-ounce packages frozen peas with onions
Seasoned pepper	Parsley sprigs
4 cups diagonally-sliced carrots	

Day before:
Pour barbecue marinade into 13-by-9-by-2-inch baking dish; lay steak in dish. Refrigerate 24 hours, turning steak several times.

About 2 hours before serving:

1. Start heating oven to 375°F.

2. Drain marinade from steak (reserve to use another day); sprinkle steak with seasoned salt and pepper. Insert roast-meat thermometer in center of steak; place on rack in broiler pan.

3. Roast 1 hour and 45 minutes, or until thermometer reads rare—140°F.

4. About 20 minutes before steak is done, start cooking carrots. When carrots are tender-crisp, stir in ginger and some butter. Also heat beets in their own liquid, drain and add some butter; cook peas with onions as package label directs.

5. Place steak on large wooden draining platter; garnish with hot vegetables and parsley. To serve, cut completely around bones; remove them. Then slice steak, in thin diagonal slices, across grain. Makes 12 servings.

STEAK WITH ONION-SPIRALED POTATO DOMES
(Pictured opposite)

1 very large Bermuda onion	2 tablespoons Worcestershire
1 tablespoon butter or margarine	1 8-serving package instant mashed potatoes
¼ teaspoon salt	Fresh dill or water cress
⅛ teaspoon pepper	
1 porterhouse steak, 1½ inches thick	

About 45 minutes before serving:

1. Preheat broiler 10 minutes, or as manufacturer directs.

2. Peel, then cut onion into ½-inch-thick slices. In jelly-roll pan lay 5 onion slices. Dot with butter; sprinkle with salt and pepper.

3. Broil on one side 6 minutes; then with spatula, turn and broil on other side 6 to 10 minutes, or until tender-crisp; keep warm while steak broils.

4. Trim surplus fat from steak; with sharp knife, slash fat edge at 2-inch intervals all around. In 12-by-8-by-2-inch pan place 1 tablespoon Worcestershire; lay steak on top, then spread with rest of Worcestershire.

5. Rub broiler rack with bit of fat trimmed from steak; remove steak from pan to rack. Broil, with top of steak 3 or 4 inches from heat, 9 to 13 minutes, depending on desired doneness. Turn steak with tongs (to avoid piercing meat); broil same time on second side.

6. While steak broils, prepare mashed potatoes as package label directs. When steak is done, remove to platter; place 5 mounds of potatoes alongside. With spatula, place onion slice on each potato mound, then press down to make spiral effect. Garnish platter with dill. Makes 5 generous servings.

CREOLE POT ROAST

1 4-pound chuck roast, without bone	1 15-ounce can tomato sauce
2 tablespoons salad oil	4 dashes Tabasco
¾ cup sliced stuffed olives	¼ teaspoon Worcestershire
	2 cups sliced onions
	Flour (optional)

About 3 hours and 30 minutes before serving:

1. Trim fat from chuck. In hot salad oil, in Dutch

Steak with Onion-Spiraled Potato Domes

oven, brown chuck well on both sides. Drain olives, reserving liquid. Add tomato sauce, ¼ cup olive liquid, Tabasco, Worcestershire, onions, and olives. Bring to boil; then simmer, tightly covered, about 3 hours, or until fork-tender.

2. Remove chuck, onions, and olives to heated platter. If thicker gravy is desired, stir 1 to 2 tablespoons flour into ¼ cup cold water; stir this paste into gravy; bring to boil, stirring; skim well. Pour some of gravy over pot roast; pass rest.

3. Nice served with hot, fluffy rice, whole-kernel corn, peach-cheese salad, and butterscotch sundaes. Makes 6 to 8 servings.

BEEF IN ORANGE JUICE

3 cloves garlic, minced	1 3-pound rump or eye-of-
¾ teaspoon cumin	round roast
¾ teaspoon ground cloves	1 onion
½ teaspoon freshly-ground	1 carrot
black pepper	1 celery stalk
Salt	2½ cups orange juice
	1 orange, sliced

Day before:

1. Mash garlic with cumin, cloves, pepper, and 1½ teaspoons salt to a paste. With sharp-pointed knife make deep cuts in meat; into each cut insert some of paste until all has been used.

2. In large kettle of salted water place meat, onion, carrot, and celery; simmer, covered, about 3 hours, or until fork-tender. Remove to plate; refrigerate overnight.

Next day:

1. Slice meat thinly; place in large shallow pan; over it pour orange juice. Let stand until serving time, turning meat occasionally.

2. To serve: Sprinkle meat with salt, if desired. Garnish with orange slices. Makes 8 servings.

BEEF AND APPLE BIRDS

⅓ cup regular all-purpose	¼ cup finely-chopped
flour	celery
Salt	1 cup chopped, pared apple
¼ teaspoon pepper	2 teaspoons prepared
1 to 1¼ pounds round	mustard
steak, ½-inch thick	¼ teaspoon sage
1 cup small fresh bread	Apple juice
crumbs	2 tablespoons shortening
¼ cup raisins	

About 2 hours and 30 minutes before serving:

1. Combine flour, 1½ teaspoons salt, and pepper; with edge of plate pound this mixture into steak, then cut steak crosswise into 5 or 6 pieces.

2. Mix crumbs, raisins, celery, apple, mustard, sage, ½ teaspoon salt, and 1 tablespoon apple juice. Spread

about ⅓ cup of this mixture on each piece of steak; roll up each and fasten with toothpick.

3. In hot shortening, in skillet, brown steak rolls on all sides. Add 1 cup apple juice; simmer, covered, 1 hour and 30 minutes, or until fork-tender. Remove picks, then serve. Makes 3 or 4 servings.

PIMENTO BEEF À LA JENSEN

1½ pounds round steak,	1 cup water or broth
without bone	1 10½-ounce can con-
Instant meat tenderizer.	densed tomato soup,
¼ cup regular all-purpose	undiluted
flour	1 cup commercial sour
¾ teaspoon salt	cream
¼ teaspoon pepper	1 4-ounce can or jar
¼ teaspoon paprika	pimentos, drained
⅓ cup salad oil	Snipped fresh dill or
1 cup thinly-sliced onions	parsley
1 pound fresh mushrooms,	
sliced	

About 1 hour before serving:

1. Treat meat with tenderizer as label directs; then cut into strips 2 inches by ¼ inch; toss in flour mixed with salt, pepper, and paprika. In hot salad oil, in deep skillet or Dutch oven, brown meat strips.

2. Reduce heat; add onions and mushrooms and cook 5 minutes. Stir in water, scraping skillet to loosen and dissolve flavorful brown bits. Cook, covered, over low heat, about 30 to 40 minutes, or until meat is fork-tender.

3. Now stir in combined soup and sour cream, then simmer to heat through (do not boil).

4. Just before removing from heat to serve, gently stir in pimentos, cut into bite-size pieces. Sprinkle with snipped dill. Serve over toast points, hot, fluffy rice, or mashed potatoes. Makes 6 servings.

SWISS STEAK WITH RAISIN GRAVY

1½ pounds round or rump	1½ cups canned tomatoes
steak, about 1 inch	3 large onions, thinly
thick	sliced
2 tablespoons regular all-	1 stalk celery, diced
purpose flour	1 clove garlic, minced
1 teaspoon salt	1 tablespoon bottled thick
⅛ teaspoon pepper	meat sauce
2 tablespoons salad oil or	¼ cup dark seedless raisins
fat	

About 2 hours and 30 minutes before serving:

1. Trim excess fat from steak. Combine flour, salt, and pepper. Lay steak on board; sprinkle with half of flour mixture, then, with edge of plate, pound in *well*. Turn meat; repeat with rest of flour mixture. Now cut meat into 6 equal serving pieces.

2. In hot salad oil, in heavy skillet or Dutch oven,

over medium heat, brown steak very well on both sides —about 15 to 20 minutes.

3. Add tomatoes, onions, celery, garlic, meat sauce, and raisins. Simmer, covered, about 2 hours, or until meat is fork-tender; add ½ cup water, if needed; skim off fat.

At serving time:

Arrange steak on heated platter, with sauce over and around it. Nice with mashed potatoes, broccoli, and tomato quarters on water cress, with poundcake and cling peaches for dessert. Makes about 6 servings.

ORIENTAL STEAK
(Pictured on page 16)

2 pounds lean chuck steak, 1¼ to 1½ inches thick	4½ cups hot fluffy rice
	1 large onion
Seasoned instant meat tenderizer	2 cups celery, in long thin strips
1 tablespoon salad oil	1 8-ounce package frozen Chinese pea pods (snow peas), thawed
1 tablespoon bottled sauce for gravy	
1 teaspoon salt	1 tablespoon cornstarch
2 teaspoons soy sauce	2 tablespoons water
1 10½-ounce can condensed consommé, undiluted	2 small red tomatoes
	Snipped parsley

About 1 hour before serving:

1. Treat steak with tenderizer as label directs. Then cut diagonally, across grain, into very thin slices, slanting knife from top to bottom.

2. In hot salad oil, in skillet, brown steak strips, adding bottled sauce for gravy. Now add salt, soy sauce, and consommé. Simmer, covered, 30 minutes, or until steak is fork-tender.

3. Meanwhile, start cooking rice. Slice onion thinly. Lay onion rings and celery on top of steak, then cook, covered, over medium heat, 5 minutes. Add thawed pea pods, then cook 2 minutes.

4. Blend cornstarch with water, then stir into liquid around steak to thicken it slightly. Add tomato wedges here and there. Remove from heat; keep warm in skillet. Stir snipped parsley into hot, fluffy rice.

5. Serve steak in skillet; pass rice. Makes 6 servings.

ZESTY BEEF BRISKET

1 4-pound beef brisket	2 tablespoons brown sugar
2 teaspoons salt	1 tablespoon Worcestershire
½ teaspoon pepper	½ cup catchup
1 medium onion, sliced	¼ cup packaged dried bread crumbs
1 teaspoon instant coffee powder	

About 4 hours before serving:

1. Place brisket in kettle or Dutch oven; add salt, pepper, onion, then cold water to cover. Bring to boil, then simmer, covered, 3 to 4 hours, or until brisket is fork-tender.

2. Start heating oven to 350°F.

3. In small bowl combine instant coffee, brown sugar, Worcestershire, and catchup.

4. When tender, remove brisket from liquid; scrape off all fat, then place in shallow baking dish. Spread with catchup mixture, then sprinkle with crumbs.

5. Bake 15 minutes.

6. Serve, sliced, with frozen chopped broccoli, potato puffs, jellied cranberry salad, refrigerated biscuits, and apple brown betty. Makes 6 to 8 servings.

CARBONNADE OF BEEF
(Pictured on page 8)

1 6-pound fresh beef brisket, without bone	1½ cups beer (12-ounce can)
Seasoned instant meat tenderizer	Dash pepper
	½ teaspoon cinnamon
1 onion, sliced	⅓ cup liquid honey
¼ cup water	¼ cup brown sugar
1 cup dried prunes	12 medium potatoes, pared and sliced
1 cup dried apricots	
¼ teaspoon ginger	

Day before:

1. Treat meat with tenderizer as label directs. With 2-tined fork, deeply pierce meat all over. Let stand at room temperature 1 hour.

2. In large Dutch oven, brown beef well on all sides in its own fat. Add onion and brown lightly. Then add water; simmer, covered, 1 hour. Cool; refrigerate in Dutch oven overnight.

3. In small bowl place prunes and apricots; sprinkle with ginger. Pour on beer; cover; refrigerate overnight.

Next day, about 1 hour and 30 minutes before serving:

1. Lift beef out of liquid; cut into slices. Skim fat from surface of liquid. Return beef slices to Dutch oven; add pepper, cinnamon, honey, and brown sugar. Simmer, covered, over low heat, 45 minutes. Then gently arrange meat slices, one on top of the other, in one half of Dutch oven. In other half alternate 3 layers of potato slices with 2 layers of fruit. Pour beer over all.

2. Simmer, covered, 30 minutes, or until potatoes are

fork-tender. Serve right from Dutch oven, or arrange in casserole or serving dish as pictured. Nice with spinach salad, lemon chiffon pie, and coffee. Makes 12 servings.

DEVILISH SHORT RIBS

3 pounds beef short ribs, cut into ribs	1 cup dried apricots
¼ cup regular all-purpose flour	2 tablespoons brown sugar
	2 tablespoons vinegar
1 10½-ounce can condensed beef broth, undiluted	¼ teaspoon cinnamon
	¼ teaspoon ground cloves
	¼ teaspoon allspice
	1 teaspoon salt

About 3 hours before serving:

1. Roll ribs in flour, then brown on all sides in hot Dutch oven. Pour off all drippings.

2. Combine beef broth, apricots, brown sugar, vinegar, cinnamon, cloves, allspice, and salt; pour over ribs. Simmer, covered, over low heat, 2½ to 3 hours, or until ribs are fork-tender, turning them and basting with sauce often.

3. Serve with buttered mixed zucchini and summer squash, potato-and-pea salad, and strawberry shortcake. Makes 6 servings.

INDOOR BARBECUED SHORT RIBS

3 pounds beef short-rib chunks	2 tablespoons cornstarch
1 tablespoon bottled sauce for gravy	1 8-ounce can tomato sauce
	½ cup water
2 tablespoons shortening or fat	1 teaspoon salt
	⅛ teaspoon pepper
1 clove garlic, minced	⅛ teaspoon allspice
½ cup minced onion	1 tablespoon prepared mustard
½ cup minced celery	1 tablespoon vinegar

1. Brush short-rib chunks with bottled sauce for gravy. In hot shortening, in Dutch oven, brown short ribs well; remove.

2. In same shortening, sauté garlic, onion, and celery until tender. Stir in cornstarch; add tomato sauce, water, salt, pepper, allspice, mustard, and vinegar; then add short ribs. Simmer, covered, 1 hour and 30 minutes, or until fork-tender. Makes 4 servings.

Carbonnade of Beef

VINEYARD BEEF SHORT RIBS

⅓ cup regular all-purpose
  flour
1 teaspoon salt
⅛ teaspoon pepper
1 teaspoon paprika

3 pounds beef short ribs,
  cut into serving pieces
¼ cup butter or margarine
1 large onion, chopped
½ bay leaf
1 beef-bouillon cube

About 2 hours and 45 minutes before serving:
1. In medium bowl combine flour, salt, pepper, and paprika. Dip meat in flour mixture, covering all sides well. Reserve leftover flour for gravy.
2. In Dutch oven, melt butter. Add short ribs and brown well on all sides. Add onion; cook until browned. Now stir in 1 cup water. Cover and cook slowly over low heat 1 hour. Add bay leaf; continue cooking about 1 hour, or until ribs are fork-tender.
3. Remove ribs from Dutch oven and place on warm platter in warm oven while making gravy.
4. For gravy: Remove bay leaf and all surface fat from drippings in Dutch oven. Stir in 1 tablespoon reserved flour, then 1 cup water, and bouillon cube. Bring to boil, stirring constantly, then cook until bouillon cube has dissolved and gravy has thickened.
5. Now remove ribs from oven and pour gravy over them. Serve immediately with rice or noodles, or fluffy mashed potatoes, buttered baby beets, wilted lettuce salad, and upside-down peach cake. Makes 4 servings.

OLD-WORLD GOULASH

Butter or margarine
4 pounds boned chuck,
  trimmed of fat and cut
  into 2-inch pieces
¼ cup white wine
1 cup canned condensed
  bouillon, undiluted
3 medium onions, minced
1 tablespoon paprika
1 teaspoon salt

1 1-pound 1-ounce can
  tomatoes
1 bay leaf
1 slice rye bread
3 cups hot instant mashed
  potatoes
1 egg, beaten
1 tablespoon commercial
  sour cream
1 tablespoon snipped
  parsley

About 3 hours before serving:
1. In ¼ cup hot butter, in large skillet, sauté chuck until nicely browned on all sides; transfer meat to large Dutch oven.
2. Into same skillet stir wine; simmer 5 minutes; add bouillon, bring to boil, then add to meat.
3. In same skillet melt 2 tablespoons butter; sauté onions until soft. Stir in paprika, salt, tomatoes, and bay leaf; simmer 5 minutes, then stir into meat.
4. In small bowl, with fork, mash rye bread with a little hot liquid from meat; blend into meat mixture. Simmer, covered, about 1 hour and 30 minutes, or until meat is fork-tender. Discard bay leaf.

5. Meanwhile, prepare mashed potatoes; while still hot, blend in egg, sour cream, 2 tablespoons melted butter, and parsley.
6. To serve, on large platter make ring of mashed potatoes; fill center with goulash. Makes 6 servings.

SAILOR'S BEEF

2 pounds chuck, without
  bone
1 teaspoon instant meat
  tenderizer
2 teaspoons salt
¼ teaspoon pepper
Butter or margarine
2 large onions, sliced

2 teaspoons prepared
  mustard
8 medium potatoes, pared,
  thinly sliced
1½ cups (12-ounce can)
  beer
Snipped parsley

About 2 hours and 30 minutes before serving:
1. Cut meat into slices ¼ inch thick; with edge of plate, pound meat slices well. Treat with tenderizer as label directs. Mix salt and pepper. In large skillet, melt 2 tablespoons butter; brown onion and meat slices, adding 1 tablespoon butter if needed; stir in mustard.
2. Start heating oven to 375°F.
3. In 3-quart casserole, arrange alternate layers of potato, onion, and meat slices, seasoning each layer with some of salt-and-pepper mixture, and ending with potato slices. Into drippings in skillet, pour ¼ cup water; bring to boil; pour water and beer over casserole.
4. Bake, covered, 1 hour and 15 minutes; then, uncover, and bake 15 minutes longer, or until meat and potatoes are tender. Sprinkle with parsley. Makes 6 to 8 servings.

BEEF STEW WITH LIMAS

⅓ cup butter or margarine
1 large onion, minced
2 pounds chuck, cut in
  2-inch pieces
1 1-pound 3-ounce can
  tomatoes

1 whole cinnamon stick
1½ teaspoons salt
½ teaspoon pepper
1 10-ounce package frozen
  Fordhook limas, thawed

Day before, or early on day:
1. In hot butter, in Dutch oven, sauté onion until golden. Add chuck and brown lightly.
2. Now add tomatoes, cinnamon stick, salt, and pepper; simmer, covered, 1½ hours, or until meat is fork-tender. Skim off fat; refrigerate stew, covered.
About 30 minutes before serving:
1. Remove any surface fat from stew. Heat stew 10 minutes, or until bubbling hot. Now add limas and cook, covered, 15 to 20 minutes, or until limas are tender.
2. Serve stew piping hot, with tossed Parmesan salad, Melba toast, and do-ahead baked apples with orange sauce. Makes 6 servings.

ITALIAN HUNTER'S STEW
(Pictured opposite)

3 tablespoons salad oil
2 pounds chuck, cut in
   2-inch pieces
2 cloves garlic, minced
3 large onions, quartered
1 6-ounce can tomato paste
1 tablespoon regular all-
   purpose flour
1 teaspoon chili powder
1 teaspoon orégano
1 teaspoon rosemary

1½ tablespoons seasoned
   salt
2 16-ounce cans stewed
   tomatoes
½ cup snipped parsley
3 medium carrots, cut into
   1-inch slices
½ pound ziti macaroni
⅓ cup shredded Parmesan
   cheese

About 2 hours and 30 minutes before serving:
1. In large Dutch oven heat salad oil; brown chuck lightly on all sides; add garlic and onions and sauté well, turning frequently.
2. Now stir in tomato paste, flour, chili powder, orégano, rosemary, seasoned salt, tomatoes, and parsley. Add 1 cup water; simmer, covered, 1 hour and 15 minutes. Skim off fat if necessary.
3. Now add carrots and simmer 45 minutes longer, or until carrots are tender.
4. Meanwhile, cook macaroni as label directs; drain well, then stir into stew with Parmesan cheese.
5. Transfer to serving dish. Serve with tossed, mixed green salad and crisp Italian bread. Makes about 6 servings.

CORNED BEEF, VIRGINIA STYLE
(Pictured on page 59)

1 8-pound corned-beef
   brisket
About 2 teaspoons whole
   cloves
1 cup light-brown sugar
½ cup packaged dried
   bread crumbs
1 teaspoon dry mustard

¼ cup coarsely-grated
   orange peel
2 tablespoons coarsely-
   grated lemon peel
½ cup orange juice
¼ cup lemon juice
1 cup apple juice

Day before:
In large kettle or Dutch oven, cover brisket with cold water. Bring to boil; simmer, covered, about 4 hours, or until fork-tender. Cool; refrigerate in cooking liquid overnight.
About 1 hour and 45 minutes before serving:
1. Start heating oven to 350°F.
2. Drain brisket; score top as in step 2 of Corned Beef, Mansion Style, below; stud with cloves; pat top with combined brown sugar, crumbs, mustard, orange and lemon peels. Place in foil-lined baking pan.
3. Bake 10 minutes; then bake 1 hour and 30 minutes, or until hot, basting often with combined orange, lemon, and apple juices.

4. In serving, slice across grain. Nice with Italian green beans, crinkle-cut French fries, and a salad of spinach tossed with purple onions and tomatoes. Makes about 12 servings.
FOR 6: Halve all ingredients; simmer about 3 hours, then bake about 1 hour.

CORNED BEEF, NEW-ENGLAND STYLE

1 7- to 8-pound corned-
   beef brisket
1 large onion, sliced
6 whole cloves
4 whole peppercorns
1 bay leaf
½ teaspoon rosemary
1 clove garlic

1 stalk celery, cut up
1 carrot, sliced
2 parsley sprigs
12 new potatoes
12 whole carrots
1 large head cabbage, cut
   in 6 wedges
2 16-ounce cans whole beets

About 5 hours and 30 minutes before serving:
1. Place corned beef in large kettle; cover with cold water; add onion, cloves, peppercorns, bay leaf, rosemary, garlic, celery, sliced carrot, and parsley. Bring to boil, then simmer, covered, 4 to 5 hours, or until meat is fork-tender.
2. Remove corned beef to large heated platter and keep warm.
3. Strain liquid from kettle; return 6 cups liquid to kettle. Then add potatoes and whole carrots. Place cabbage on top of them. Bring to boil, then simmer, covered, 30 minutes, or until vegetables are just tender-crisp.
4. Meanwhile, in saucepan, heat beets.
5. Slice meat, then arrange drained vegetables around it. Pass mustard pickles, chili sauce, or horse-radish. Makes 12 servings.
FOR 6: Use a 3½- to 4-pound corned-beef brisket; halve all other ingredients. Cook as in step 1 for 3 to 4 hours, or until tender. Then proceed as directed.

CORNED BEEF, MANSION STYLE
(Pictured on page 12)

1 8½-pound corned-beef
   brisket
3 onion slices
Whole cloves

6 whole peppercorns
1 bay leaf
½ teaspoon rosemary
Light-brown sugar

About 5 hours before serving:
1. Place corned beef in large deep kettle; cover completely with cold water. Add onion slices, each studded with 4 whole cloves, peppercorns, bay leaf, and rosemary. Bring to boil; simmer, covered, about 4 hours, or until fork-tender.
2. About 10 minutes before corned beef is done, remove it to large shallow pan. With sharp knife make diagonal cuts, ⅛ inch deep and about ¾ inch apart, across entire top surface. Repeat, at an angle, to make

Italian Hunter's Stew, Sumptuous Chicken Stew

a series of squares or diamonds. Stud these squares with whole cloves. Pat on brown sugar, ⅛ inch thick.
3.   Next, in preheated broiler, broil corned beef until brown-sugar surface is nicely glazed.
4.   Serve sliced, with baked sweet potatoes and skillet-cooked, sliced cabbage. Makes about 8 servings.

ROLLED MEAT LOAF AU GOURMET
(Pictured on page 16)

1 tablespoon butter or
  margarine
½ cup diced celery
1 medium onion, minced
1½ pounds chuck, ground
½ cup packaged dried bread
  crumbs

1 egg, unbeaten
1½ teaspoons salt
1 tablespoon Worcester-
  shire
2 frankfurters
8 slices bacon

About 50 minutes before serving:
1.   In hot butter, in skillet, sauté celery and onion until tender, stirring occasionally.
2.   Meanwhile, in bowl combine chuck with crumbs, egg, salt, and Worcestershire. Add celery-and-onion mixture; stir all together, with 2-tined fork, until just blended. Place this mixture on strip of wax paper 14 by 12 inches. Pat it into rectangle 12 by 10 inches.
3.   Cut each frankfurter into four lengthwise strips; place these strips, about 1-inch apart, and parallel to short side of meat, down length of meat. Then move every other frankfurter to opposite edge.
4.   Now, with aid of wax paper, roll up meat tightly, from short side, jelly-roll fashion, with frankfurters as filling. Lay 2 bacon slices, side by side, along top of roll; lay 6 bacon slices across these two so they girdle roll; secure ends of bacon with toothpicks.
5.   Sauté meat roll on all sides on medium-hot griddle, or in oval Dutch oven or 12-inch skillet, for 30 minutes, or until bacon is brown and meat done, using pancake turner and spatula to turn it as needed. Let stand 10 minutes.
6.   Cut into thick slices. Serve with asparagus spears, marinated tomato slices, Melba toast, and lemon-chiffon pie topped with blueberries. Makes 6 to 8 servings.

Corned Beef, Mansion Style

LEMON BARBECUED BEEF LOAVES

1½ pounds chuck, ground
3 tablespoons lemon juice
1 tablespoon water
⅓ cup fresh bread crumbs
Seasoned salt
¼ teaspoon seasoned
    pepper
⅓ cup catchup
¼ teaspoon prepared
    mustard
⅛ teaspoon ground cloves
¼ teaspoon Worcestershire
6 lemon slices

About 30 minutes before serving:
1.   Start heating oven to 450°F.
2.   Combine ground chuck, 2 tablespoons lemon juice, water, crumbs, ½ teaspoon seasoned salt, and seasoned pepper. Form into 6 individual meat loaves, each approximately 3 by 2 by 1 inch. Arrange in 10-by-6-by-2-inch baking dish.
3.   Bake about 5 minutes; meanwhile, combine catchup, mustard, cloves, Worcestershire, 1 tablespoon lemon juice, and ¼ teaspoon seasoned salt.
4.   Remove loaves from oven; spoon catchup mixture over them, then top each with lemon slice. Bake about 10 minutes longer, or until brown all over, but moist within.
5.   Remove from oven, arrange on warm platter and serve. Makes 6 servings.

SUKIYAKI MEAT BALLS

1 pound chuck, ground
½ cup packaged dried
    bread crumbs
½ cup chopped onion
1 teaspoon salt
⅛ teaspoon pepper
1 6-ounce can evaporated
    milk, undiluted
1 egg, unbeaten
2 tablespoons salad oil
1 1-pound can bean sprouts
1 3- or 4-ounce can sliced
    mushrooms
¼ cup cornstarch
¼ cup soy sauce
1½ cups thinly-sliced
    onions
1 10-ounce package frozen
    chopped spinach, thawed
6 cups hot cooked rice

About 45 minutes before serving:
1.   Combine chuck, crumbs, chopped onion, salt, pepper, milk, and egg; shape into 12 balls.
2.   In large skillet, in hot oil, brown meat balls on all sides. Meanwhile, drain bean sprouts, reserving liquid; to reserved liquid add enough water to measure 2 cups.
3.   Drain mushrooms, reserving liquid; mix ¼ cup reserved mushroom liquid with cornstarch to make a smooth paste. Stir into bean-sprout liquid; add soy sauce and mix well. Pour over browned meat balls. Bring to boil; then simmer, covered, 10 minutes.
4.   Now pile meat balls to one side of skillet; add sliced onions; simmer, covered, 5 minutes. Add mushrooms, bean sprouts, and spinach; simmer, covered, 5 minutes.
5.   Serve meat-ball mixture over bed of hot rice. Nice with spiced peaches. Makes 6 servings.

BEEF BALLS IN ZESTY SAUCE

1½ pounds chuck, ground
1 cup fresh whole-wheat
    bread crumbs
¼ cup undiluted evaporated
    milk
2 teaspoons Worcestershire
1 teaspoon sage
Salt
2 tablespoons shortening
2 medium onions, sliced
1 cup applesauce
1 tablespoon prepared
    horse-radish
½ cup canned tomato sauce
⅛ teaspoon orégano
⅛ teaspoon pepper
1 tablespoon lemon juice

About 45 minutes before serving:
1.   Combine chuck, crumbs, evaporated milk, Worcestershire, sage, and 1½ teaspoons salt; mix well; shape into 1½-inch balls.
2.   In hot shortening, in large skillet, brown beef balls on all sides; pile to one side of skillet. Now, in same skillet, sauté onions until golden. To them add applesauce, horse-radish, tomato sauce, orégano, 1 teaspoon salt, pepper, and lemon juice; heat thoroughly, then serve. Nice with green beans, sweet potatoes, coleslaw, and gelatin dessert. Makes 6 servings.

BUFFET MEAT BALLS IN BURGUNDY
(Pictured on page 15)

3 pounds chuck, ground
3 cups packaged dried
    bread crumbs, or finely-
    crushed cornflakes
2 large onions, minced
1 tablespoon cornstarch
¼ teaspoon allspice
4 eggs, beaten
3 cups light cream
Salt
½ cup salad oil or
    shortening
1 cup regular all-purpose
    flour
6 cups water
3¾ cups Burgundy
8 beef-bouillon cubes
½ teaspoon pepper
2 tablespoons granulated
    sugar
Bottled sauce for gravy

Day before, if desired:
1.   Combine chuck, crumbs, onions, cornstarch, allspice, eggs, cream, and 1 tablespoon salt; shape into 1-inch balls.
2.   Into hot salad oil, in large Dutch oven, drop meat balls, a few at a time; brown on all sides, then transfer to tray or cookie sheet.
3.   For sauce: Stir flour into oil remaining in Dutch oven; stir in water, Burgundy, bouillon cubes, 1 teaspoon salt, pepper, sugar, and enough bottled sauce for gravy to make light brown. Cook, stirring, until smooth. Arrange meat balls in sauce; simmer, covered, 30 minutes. Cool; refrigerate.
At serving time:
Reheat meat balls in sauce; turn into 4-quart chafing dish; set on buffet. (If using 2-quart chafing dish, keep half of mixture hot in Dutch oven for second helpings.) Makes 20 servings.

BEEF PINWHEELS
(Pictured opposite)

1 4-serving envelope instant mashed potatoes
3 tablespoons grated Parmesan cheese
¼ teaspoon orégano
1 10-ounce package frozen peas
2 pounds chuck, ground
1 egg, unbeaten
½ cup packaged dried bread crumbs
1½ teaspoons seasoned salt
½ teaspoon seasoned pepper
1 10-ounce can beef gravy

Day before:
1. Prepare instant mashed potatoes as package label directs; then add cheese and orégano. Cook peas half the time label directs; cool potatoes and peas.
2. In medium bowl combine chuck with egg, crumbs, seasoned salt and pepper. Turn meat onto long piece of foil; firmly pat to rectangle 15½ by 8 inches, keeping edges straight. Spread potatoes over meat, covering an area of 12 by 7 inches, thus leaving ½ inch on each side and 3 inches at one end unspread. Over potatoes spread peas. Then, starting at 8-inch end, firmly roll up meat, jelly-roll fashion. Refrigerate, covered.
About 50 minutes before serving:
1. Start heating oven to 350°F.
2. Lay meat, seam side down, in roasting pan; remove foil; pat into shape.
3. Bake 45 minutes, or until a rich brown. Then, with wide spatula and pancake turner transfer to warm platter. Serve, sliced, with hot gravy. Makes about 10 to 12 servings.
Note: To make, bake same day, allow 1 hour and 15 minutes.

SCANDINAVIAN BURGERS

2 eggs, unbeaten
1½ pounds chuck, ground
1½ cups soft day-old bread crumbs
1 medium onion, chopped
1 teaspoon salt
¼ teaspoon pepper
1 teaspoon Worcestershire
Flour
2 tablespoons salad oil or shortening
1 10½-ounce can condensed cream-of-mushroom soup, undiluted
¾ cup water
¼ teaspoon allspice or nutmeg

About 35 minutes before serving:
1. In medium bowl, with 2-tined fork, beat eggs slightly; add chuck, crumbs, onion, salt, pepper, and Worcestershire; mix with fork until well blended. Shape into 6 to 8 oval-shaped patties. Roll in a little flour; brown in hot salad oil in skillet.
2. Beat together soup, water, and allspice; add to burgers in skillet. Simmer, covered, 20 minutes. Makes 6 to 8 servings.
FOR 3 OR 4: Halve all ingredients; make as above.

HAMBURGER ROLLS

½ pound chuck, ground
½ cup fine fresh bread crumbs
¼ cup milk
1½ teaspoons lemon juice
¼ cup finely-grated Cheddar cheese
2 tablespoons chopped stuffed olives
½ teaspoon salt
3 bacon slices

1. Combine chuck, crumbs, milk, lemon juice, cheese, olives, and salt.
2. Start heating oven to 400°F.
3. Divide chuck mixture into thirds. Shape each third into a roll 4 by 1½ inches; wrap each in a bacon slice. Lay rolls in 8-inch pie plate.
4. Bake 30 minutes, then broil 2 minutes to crisp bacon. Makes 2 or 3 servings.

STROGANOFF SKILLET DINNER

2 tablespoons salad oil or shortening
½ pound chuck, ground
1 small onion, chopped
1½ cups uncooked medium noodles
1½ cups canned tomato juice
1 teaspoon Worcestershire
1 teaspoon celery salt
½ teaspoon salt
Dash pepper
½ cup commercial sour cream
Snipped parsley

1. In hot salad oil in skillet brown chuck and onion, stirring occasionally.
2. Over browned meat mixture lay noodles. Pour on tomato juice mixed with Worcestershire, celery salt, salt, and pepper. Simmer, covered, 25 minutes, stirring occasionally, or until noodles are tender.
3. Stir in sour cream; sprinkle with parsley. Makes 3 servings.

TOMATO-CHEESEBURGER PIE

½ package piecrust mix (1 stick)
1½ pounds lean chuck, ground
1 tablespoon instant minced onion
⅓ cup packaged dried bread crumbs
¼ teaspoon pepper
Dash Tabasco
¼ cup catchup
½ teaspoon garlic salt
1½ teaspoons seasoned salt
1 egg, beaten
1 medium tomato, cut into ½-inch slices
½ cup grated process Cheddar cheese

About 45 minutes before serving:
1. Prepare piecrust mix as package label directs for 9-inch pie shell, having a fluted edge.
2. Start heating oven to 425°F.
3. In medium bowl combine chuck, onion, crumbs, pepper, Tabasco, catchup, garlic salt, seasoned salt, and egg, mixing until well blended.

Beef Pinwheels

Buffet Meat Balls in Burgundy

Oriental Steak, Meat Loaf au Gourm

Broiler-Style Dinner, Hamburger-Macaroni Trea

4. Spread this mixture over bottom of unbaked pie shell, then arrange tomato slices on top in a circle, overlapping slightly.

5. Bake 25 minutes, or until meat reaches desired doneness.

6. Now sprinkle tomatoes with cheese, return pie to oven for 2 minutes, or until cheese is melted. Serve, cut into wedges. Makes 6 servings.

MEXICAN CHILI

2 tablespoons salad oil or shortening	¾ cup boiling water
½ cup thinly-sliced onions	1¼ cups canned tomatoes
¾ pound chuck, ground once	½ teaspoon salt
	1 teaspoon granulated sugar
1 to 1½ tablespoons chili powder	1½ small cloves garlic, minced
2 tablespoons cold water	1 16-ounce can kidney beans

About 1 hour and 45 minutes before serving:

1. In skillet, in hot oil, sauté onions and chuck until meat loses red color.

2. Combine chili powder with water; stir into meat. Add boiling water, tomatoes, salt, sugar, and garlic; simmer, covered, 1 hour.

3. Uncover; simmer 30 minutes. Skim off fat if necessary. Add kidney beans; heat. Makes 3 servings.

HAMBURGER-MACARONI TREAT
(Pictured opposite)

4 large green peppers	½ teaspoon nutmeg
1 large onion, chopped	¼ cup milk
2 pounds chuck, ground	¼ cup salad oil or shortening
1 cup cooked rice	
¼ cup snipped parsley	2 eggs, well beaten
Salt	2 15-ounce cans macaroni and cheese
Pepper	
2 tablespoons prepared horse-radish	4 large red tomatoes
	Worcestershire
1 teaspoon prepared mustard	Paprika
	Water cress

About 1 hour before serving:

1. Cut tops from green peppers; remove seeds. Then boil in boiling salted water, covered, 5 minutes; drain.

2. Start heating oven to 350°F.

3. In bowl combine onion, chuck, rice, parsley, 1 teaspoon salt, ¼ teaspoon pepper, horse-radish, mustard, nutmeg, and milk. Divide mixture in half; then cook half of it in hot oil in skillet until meat loses red color. Use of fill pepper shells. Arrange down one side of 13-by-9-by-2-inch baking dish.

4. To remaining meat mixture add beaten eggs; shape into tiny meat balls; sauté in 2 tablespoons hot oil in same skillet until brown. Top each filled pepper with 3 meat balls; place remaining meat balls down center of baking dish.

5. Bake meat balls and peppers 15 minutes.

6. Meanwhile, heat macaroni and cheese in saucepan. Scoop out center of tomatoes; season with salt, pepper, and Worcestershire, then fill with hot macaroni; sprinkle with paprika. Arrange beside peppers in baking dish, then return all to oven for about 8 minutes.

7. Serve right from baking dish; garnish with water cress. Makes 4 servings.

FOR 2: Halve all ingredients; use 10-by-6-by-2-inch baking dish; make and bake as above.

HAMBURGER CHOP SUEY

2 tablespoons salad oil or shortening	½ cup canned condensed bouillon, undiluted
½ pound chuck, ground	1 3- or 4-ounce can sliced mushrooms, undrained
1 small onion, sliced	
½ cup celery, in large pieces	1 tablespoon cornstarch
	2 tablespoons soy sauce
1 cup drained canned bean sprouts	Hot rice

1. In skillet, in hot oil, sauté chuck, onion, and celery until meat loses red color.

2. Add bean sprouts, bouillon, and mushrooms. Simmer, covered, 10 minutes.

3. Stir in cornstarch blended with soy sauce; simmer until thickened, stirring. Serve over hot rice. Makes 3 servings.

CHEESY CHILI

2 tablespoons butter or margarine	1½ tablespoons chili powder
1 pound lean chuck, ground	1 teaspoon orégano
1 cup minced onions	1 teaspoon salt
1 1-pound 4-ounce can kidney beans (2½ cups)	½ cup water
	½ cup chopped ripe olives
1 10½-ounce can condensed tomato soup, undiluted	½ cup grated process sharp-Cheddar cheese
	¼ cup fresh snipped parsley

About 1 hour and 45 minutes before serving:

1. In large skillet, in hot butter; cook chuck and onions, one fourth of each at a time, until brown.

2. Now, into meat mixture stir kidney beans and soup; cook about 10 minutes.

3. Next add chili powder, orégano, salt, water, and ripe olives. Cook, over low heat, stirring frequently, 45 minutes.

4. Then add cheese and stir until cheese is melted. Pour chili into heated casserole or serving dish; sprinkle top with parsley. Serve immediately with saltines or hot buttered French bread. Makes 4 servings.

Pork

The all-important rule for pork cookery: Serve pork cooked thoroughly, but not overcooked. Pork loin roasts, cooked to 170°F. internal temperature, are more juicy and cook in less time than those cooked to a higher internal temperature.

JEWELED PORK ROAST

1 6- to 8-pound pork-loin roast
1 teaspoon salt
¼ teaspoon pepper
2 tablespoons granulated sugar
1 1-pound 14-ounce can pear halves, drained
1 1-pound 14-ounce can cling-peach halves, drained
Mint jelly
Canned whole cranberry sauce
Fresh sage sprigs (optional)

About 3 hours and 15 minutes before serving:
1. Start heating oven to 325°F.
2. Place pork roast, fat side up, on rack in shallow open roasting pan; rub roast with salt, pepper, and sugar. Insert roast-meat thermometer in center of thick meaty part of roast, so it does not rest on bone.
3. Roast about 3 hours, or until thermometer registers 170°F.
4. Meanwhile, arrange drained pear and peach halves, side by side, in large baking dish; heat them in oven along with roast, during last 20 minutes.
5. When done, place roast on heated platter. Around roast arrange hot pear and peach halves. Fill pear halves with mint jelly, peach halves with cranberry sauce. Garnish with sage sprigs, if desired.
6. Serve pork roast with buttered peas and limas, celery slaw, chilled vanilla pudding, topped with chocolate sauce and peanuts. Makes 10 to 12 servings.

SWEET-PUNGENT PORK LOIN

3 large cloves garlic, crushed
6 tablespoons soy sauce
½ cup catchup
¼ cup lemon juice
½ teaspoon pepper
1 4- to 6-pound boneless pork-loin roast
2 cloves garlic, each cut into 6 slivers
18 whole cloves
2 cups apricot preserves
6 spiced crab apples

Day before:
1. In bowl combine crushed garlic cloves, soy sauce, catchup, lemon juice, and pepper to use as a marinade in step 3.
2. With sharp knife, make 12 small cuts (about ½ inch deep) into fat surface of roast; insert sliver of garlic in each. Stud remaining fat surface with whole cloves.
3. Place pork roast in 13-by-9-by-2-inch baking dish; pour soy-sauce marinade over it; cover with foil. Refrigerate roast until about 3 hours before serving, turning it in marinade several times.

About 3 hours before serving:
1. Start heating oven to 325°F.
2. Lift pork roast from marinade. Place it, with fat side up, on rack in shallow open roasting pan; baste with marinade. Insert roast-meat thermometer into center of thick meaty part of roast.
3. Roast about 1½ hours, or until roast-meat thermometer registers 160°F. Then remove pork from oven.
4. Meanwhile, heat apricot preserves until melted. Brush ½ cup of them over top of roast, reserving rest to pass as sauce. Return pork to oven and continue roasting 20 to 30 minutes, or until thermometer registers 170°F.
5. Place roast on large platter. Garnish with spiced crab apples. Serve roast with reserved heated apricot preserves. Makes 8 to 12 servings.

OVEN BARBECUED ROAST PORK
(Pictured opposite)

1 6- to 8-pound pork-loin roast
1 medium onion, chopped
⅓ cup chopped celery
1 clove garlic, minced
2 tablespoons brown sugar
2 teaspoons prepared mustard
1 10½-ounce can condensed tomato soup, undiluted
2 tablespoons Worcestershire
2 tablespoons vinegar
Dash Tabasco
2 16-ounce cans small, whole white potatoes, drained
Paprika
Parsley sprigs

About 3 hours and 15 minutes before serving:
1. Start heating oven to 325°F.
2. Place pork roast in shallow open roasting pan; insert roast-meat thermometer in center of thick meaty part of roast, so it does not rest on bone.
3. Roast, uncovered, 2 hours.
4. Meanwhile, in saucepan combine onion, celery, garlic, brown sugar, mustard, soup, Worcestershire, vinegar, and Tabasco; simmer 5 minutes.
5. Pour fat from roasting pan; arrange potatoes on one side of roast; sprinkle with paprika. Spoon some of sauce over roast; then roast 1 hour longer, or until meat thermometer registers 170°F.
6. When done, remove roast to heated platter. Spoon

Oven-Barbecued Pork Roast, Ravietti

Baked Pork Chops aux Pommes de Terre

Pork Roast with Pineapple-Yam Rose

sauce over potatoes, then arrange beside meat. Garnish with parsley. Makes 10 to 12 servings.

PORK ROAST WITH PINEAPPLE-YAM ROSETTES
(Pictured opposite)

2 16- or 17-ounce cans yams	Salt
1 1-pound 13-ounce can sliced pineapple	2 tablespoons melted butter or margarine
1 tablespoon sherry	1 6- to 8-pound pork-loin roast
¼ teaspoon ground cloves	Pepper
½ teaspoon nutmeg	½ cup instant minced onion
¼ teaspoon allspice	

About 3 hours and 15 minutes before serving:

1. Drain yams and pineapple slices, reserving liquids. Whip yams with sherry, cloves, nutmeg, all spice, ¼ teaspoon salt, and melted butter until creamy. Refrigerate yams, pineapple slices, and liquids.
2. Start heating oven to 325°F.
3. Place roast, fat side up, on rack in shallow open roasting pan; insert roast-meat thermometer into center of thick meaty part of roast, so it does not rest on bone. Rub roast well with salt, pepper, and instant minced onion.
4. Roast about 3 hours, or until meat thermometer registers 170°F., basting often with combined yam and pineapple liquids.
5. Remove pork roast to heated platter; turn oven temperature to "broil." Place pineapple slices on cookie sheet. Top each pineapple slice with a rosette of yam mixture; broil until golden. Arrange around roast. Makes 10 to 12 servings.

BAKED PORK CHOPS AUX POMMES DE TERRE
(Pictured on page 19)

6 loin or shoulder pork chops, 1 inch thick	1 package scalloped potatoes
1 teaspoon salt	⅛ teaspoon dried thyme
½ teaspoon pepper	1 12-ounce can whole-kernel corn with peppers
⅓ cup water	⅛ teaspoon chili powder

About 1 hour and 30 minutes before serving:

1. Sauté pork chops in skillet until well browned on both sides. Sprinkle them with salt and pepper; add water, then simmer, covered, 30 minutes.
2. Start heating oven to 400°F.
3. Meanwhile, prepare scalloped potatoes for baking as package label directs, adding thyme; arrange potatoes in 10-by-6-by-2-inch baking dish.
4. Lay browned chops on top of potatoes; cover with foil.

5. Bake 30 minutes.
6. Uncover chops, then stand them up back to back, in a circle on top of potatoes. Drain corn; toss with chili powder, then spoon between chops. Cover with foil.
7. Bake chops 15 minutes longer, or until corn is heated through. Makes 6 servings.

PORK CHOPS CREOLE

6 loin pork chops, 1 inch thick	½ green pepper, chopped
Unsifted regular all-purpose flour	1 teaspoon salt
	¼ teaspoon pepper
1 medium onion, chopped	1½ teaspoons Worcestershire
1 1-pound 3-ounce can tomatoes	1 cup uncooked regular white rice

About 1 hour and 30 minutes before serving:

1. Sprinkle pork chops lightly on both sides with some of flour.
2. In large skillet, sauté chops, first on fat ends, then on each side, until golden—about 10 minutes; remove and set aside to keep warm until needed.
3. Drain some of fat from skillet; in rest of fat sauté onion until golden; add tomatoes, green pepper, salt, pepper, and Worcestershire.
4. Return chops to skillet; simmer, covered, 1 hour, or until fork-tender.
5. About 20 minutes before chops are done, cook rice as package label directs.
6. When pork chops are tender, lift them from sauce and arrange on heated platter. Cover chops with rice, then pour sauce over all, skimming off fat, if necessary. Makes 6 servings.

PORK CHOPS IN MUSTARD SAUCE

4 loin pork chops, ½ inch thick	1½ cups canned beef broth
	Prepared mustard
1 teaspoon seasoned salt	⅓ cup light cream
Unsifted regular all-purpose flour	1 large dill pickle, sliced
1 tablespoon butter or margarine	Parsley sprigs

About 1 hour and 15 minutes before serving:

1. Sprinkle pork chops with seasoned salt, then coat lightly with flour.
2. In medium skillet, in hot butter, brown chops well on all sides. Pour off excess fat.
3. Beat 1 tablespoon flour with beef broth; pour over chops in skillet. Bring to boil; then simmer, covered, 45 minutes to 1 hour, or until chops are fork-tender.
4. Meanwhile, blend 1 to 1½ tablespoons mustard with cream. Add to sauce in skillet, stirring until smooth. Bring to boil; then arrange chops on warm serving plat-

ter; pour on sauce, then garnish with pickle slices and parsley. Makes 4 servings.

PORK HOCKS IN THE ROUND
(Pictured below)

2 tablespoons bottled sauce for gravy	2 1-pound 13-ounce cans sauerkraut
8 fresh pork hocks	¾ cup brown sugar
1 teaspoon salt	2 medium red cooking apples
1 cup boiling water	Granulated sugar
Lemon juice	2 tablespoons butter or margarine
1 cup chopped onions	Snipped parsley
1½ tablespoons caraway seeds	

About 3 hours before serving:

1. Combine bottled sauce for gravy with ¼ cup cold water; pour into large Dutch oven; heat. In it brown pork hocks on all sides. Add salt, boiling water, 1 tablespoon lemon juice, and onions. Simmer, covered, 1 hour and 30 minutes.

2. Now mix caraway seeds, sauerkraut, and brown sugar; lay over hocks. Simmer, covered, 50 minutes.

3. About 15 minutes before kraut is done, core apples, slice thickly, dip in lemon juice, and sprinkle with sugar. In hot butter, in skillet, sauté apple slices until golden.

4. Using slotted spoon, lift sauerkraut to heated plat-

ter; on it arrange pork hocks and apple slices. Sprinkle with parsley. Serve with instant mashed potatoes or frozen mashed-potato puffs, romaine salad, tiny wedges of cheesecake, and coffee. Makes 8 servings.

PEPPER-PORK STEW

¼ cup salad oil	¼ teaspoon crushed red pepper
2 pounds lean pork, cut into 1½-inch pieces	¼ teaspoon cinnamon
3 tablespoons uncooked regular rice	1 10½-ounce can condensed beef consommé, undiluted
4 medium onions, coarsely chopped	3 medium potatoes, pared, quartered
3 cloves garlic, minced	¼ cup chopped salted peanuts
3 medium tomatoes, coarsely chopped	¼ cup heavy cream
¼ teaspoon saffron (optional)	1 tablespoon molasses
1½ teaspoons salt	1 green banana, quartered

About 1 hour and 30 minutes before serving:

1. In hot salad oil, in large Dutch oven, brown pork on all sides; add rice, onions, and garlic; sauté 5 minutes, turning frequently. Stir in tomatoes, saffron, salt, red pepper, cinnamon, and consommé. Simmer, tightly covered, 1 hour.

2. Stir in potatoes, then simmer 15 minutes. Add peanuts, cream, molasses, and banana; simmer about 15

Pork Hocks in the Round

minutes, or until potatoes and pork are tender. Makes about 6 servings.

ORANGE PORK STROGANOFF

3 pounds boned pork shoulder	2 teaspoons seasoned salt
2 tablespoons salad oil	1 teaspoon monosodium glutamate
2 medium onions, chopped	¼ teaspoon pepper
2 tablespoons regular all-purpose flour	1 8-ounce package broad noodles
2 tablespoons grated orange peel	1 cup commercial sour cream
1 cup orange juice	Few orange sections

About 2 hours before serving:
1. Trim fat from pork; slice pork thinly, across grain. In hot salad oil, in skillet, sauté pork and onions. Stir in flour, orange peel and juice, seasoned salt, monosodium glutamate, and pepper. Simmer, covered, 1 hour, or until pork is fork-tender.
2. About 20 minutes before pork is done, cook noodles as package label directs.
3. Into tender pork stir sour cream; arrange on platter surrounded by noodles; garnish with orange sections. Serve with fresh spinach salad with favorite dressing, crisp poppy-seed rolls, and chocolate-glazed angel-food cake. Makes 4 to 6 servings.

BACON-ONION SUPPER TREAT

About 16 slices lean bacon	¼ cup shredded process Cheddar cheese
2 cups packaged biscuit mix	3 medium onions, thinly sliced
1 egg, unbeaten	Creamy Scrambled Eggs, below
¾ cup milk	
Seasoned salt	

About 1 hour before serving:
1. Fry 4 bacon slices until crisp; drain on paper towels, then crumble.
2. Start heating oven to 400°F.
3. In medium bowl combine biscuit mix, egg, and milk; then, with wooden spoon, beat hard for 30 seconds. Now fold in crumbled bacon, 1 teaspoon seasoned salt, and cheese.
4. Pour batter onto greased cookie sheet, spreading it evenly into an 11-inch circle. Spread onions over top of batter; sprinkle with ½ teaspoon seasoned salt. Over onions lay 4 rows of 4 bacon slices, lattice-style, twisting each bacon slice slightly.
5. Bake 30 minutes, or until golden and bacon is crisp, laying a piece of foil on bottom oven rack to catch any bacon drippings.
6. Toward end of baking time, start making Creamy Scrambled Eggs. Serve bacon dish, in wedges, with eggs. Makes about 8 servings.

CREAMY SCRAMBLED EGGS: Beat 8 eggs, with ¾ cup evaporated milk, undiluted, 1 teaspoon seasoned salt, ½ cup shredded process Cheddar cheese, ½ cup snipped parsley, and ⅛ teaspoon pepper. In medium skillet heat 2 tablespoons butter or margarine; in it slowly cook egg mixture, stirring occasionally, until set, but still moist. Turn out on serving dish.

HOT-TAMALE PIE

1 pound bulk pork sausage	1 clove garlic, minced
¾ cup yellow corn meal	1 8-ounce can tomato sauce
3 cups boiling water	1 to 1½ teaspoons chili powder
1 teaspoon salt	⅓ cup chopped ripe olives
3 eggs, beaten	Snipped parsley
1 medium onion, chopped	

About 1 hour and 30 minutes before serving:
1. In medium skillet cook sausage, breaking it into small pieces, until browned.
2. Meanwhile, start heating oven to 375°F.
3. Gradually stir corn meal into boiling salted water; cook, stirring constantly, 10 minutes, or until very thick. Stir cooked corn meal into beaten eggs; spoon half of this mixture into greased 9-inch pie plate, mounding against sides.
4. Drain fat from sausage; add onion and garlic; sauté 2 or 3 minutes; then stir in tomato sauce, chili powder, and olives; cook 5 minutes. Spoon sausage mixture evenly into pie plate, leaving ½ inch corn meal exposed around edge; cover sausage mixture with remaining corn-meal mixture.
5. Bake 45 minutes. Sprinkle with parsley; serve hot, in wedges. Makes 6 to 8 servings.

GLAZED SWEET-AND-SOUR PORK

3 tablespoons butter or margarine	1 cup canned crushed pineapple
¼ cup green-pepper strips	2 tablespoons vinegar
¼ cup coarsely-chopped onion	1 tablespoon soy sauce
1 tablespoon cornstarch	4 thick slices cold roast pork

About 15 minutes before serving:
1. Preheat broiler 10 minutes, or as manufacturer directs.
2. In hot butter, in skillet, sauté green-pepper strips and onion about 5 minutes; gradually stir in cornstarch, then pineapple; stir until mixture thickens. Add vinegar and soy sauce. Pour this sweet-and-sour sauce over pork slices in shallow open pan.
3. Broil, about 4½ inches from heat, 5 minutes.
4. Serve with hot, fluffy rice, or canned shoestring potatoes or Chinese noodles, hearts of lettuce with oil-and-vinegar dressing, and vanilla ice cream with peaches. Makes 4 servings.

Ham

BAKED HAM WITH CHERRIES

6 medium yams or sweet
  potatoes
Salad oil
1 slice fully-cooked ham,
  1 inch thick (about
  1½ pounds)
½ cup light or dark brown
  sugar, packed

⅛ teaspoon nutmeg
½ cup sherry
1 1-pound 1-ounce can
  pitted Bing cherries,
  drained
1 tablespoon brandy
Butter or margarine
4 thick orange slices

About 1 hour before serving:
1.   Start heating oven to 350°F.
2.   Scrub and dry yams, then rub each with a little salad oil.
3.   Bake 45 to 50 minutes, or until fork-tender.
4.   Meanwhile, place ham slice in 12-by-8-by-2-inch baking dish. Cover with brown sugar, then sprinkle with nutmeg.
5.   In bowl combine sherry, drained cherries, and brandy; pour around ham slice. Top ham slice with orange slices; then bake, along with yams, for last 30 minutes.
6.   When done, on large heated platter arrange yams. In top center of each cut a 1½-inch cross. Press bottom of each until tender interior bursts through cross. With fork, break up interior of each potato lightly; then lay piece of butter on top.
7.   Lay ham slice, cut into 6 pieces, on platter in center of baked yams, with orange slices on top. Pass cherry sauce. Makes 6 servings.

HAM 'N' YAM BAKE

½ cup chili sauce
½ cup flavored syrup
1 tablespoon vinegar
1 tablespoon melted butter
  or margarine
1 1-pound, center-cut
  ready-to-eat ham slice,
  1 inch thick

1 1-pound can cut Blue
  Lake green beans,
  drained
1 1-pound can yams,
  drained
Fresh parsley sprigs

About 50 minutes before serving:
1.   Start heating oven to 325°F.
2.   In small bowl mix together chili sauce, syrup, vinegar, and melted butter.
3.   With paring knife make a series of slashes in fat edge of ham slice to prevent curling. Brush ham with some of chili-sauce mixture; place on ovenglass platter.

4.   Bake, uncovered, 25 minutes; turn ham slice; place beans and yams on top, then brush with remaining chili-sauce mixture. Bake 15 minutes, or until heated through.
5.   Serve garnished with parsley sprigs. Makes 4 servings.

APPLE-STUFFED HAM
(Pictured opposite)

Melted butter or margarine
1 cup finely-chopped
  celery
1 large onion, finely
  chopped
1 1-pound 4-ounce can
  pie-sliced apples
1½ cups packaged herb-
  seasoned stuffing mix

¼ cup finely-snipped
  parsley
2 center-cut ham steaks,
  each ½ inch thick
2 tablespoons apricot jam
2 9-ounce packages frozen
  Italian-style green
  beans

About 1 hour and 30 minutes before serving:
1.   Start heating oven to 350°F.
2.   In 2 tablespoons melted butter, in skillet, sauté celery and onion until golden.
3.   In large bowl combine celery-onion mixture, apples, stuffing mix, and parsley; slowly add, while tossing, ½ cup melted butter.
4.   Lay one ham slice in roasting pan; top with stuffing mixture, then with second ham slice. Spread apricot jam over top.
5.   Bake 1 hour.
6.   Cook beans as label directs; season to taste.
7.   With 2 wide spatulas lift meat to warm platter; arrange beans along one side. Serve ham, cut into slices with sharp knife. Makes 6 servings.

SIZZLING HAM PLATTER

2 cups cooked or canned
  lima beans, seasoned
1 ready-to-eat ham slice
  (1¼ pounds)
⅓ cup apricot jam
2 large red apples, cored
¼ cup lemon juice

6 canned cling-peach
  halves, drained
3 bananas
2 tablespoons melted butter
  or margarine
Fresh parsley sprigs

About 30 minutes before serving:
1.   Preheat broiler 10 minutes, or as manufacturer directs.
2.   In bottom of broiler pan place lima beans; set broiler rack in place; in center lay ham slice. Spread ham lightly with some of apricot jam.
3.   Broil 10 minutes.
4.   Meanwhile, slice each apple into 3 rings; dip rings in lemon juice.
5.   Now remove broiler pan from broiler; turn ham slice. Spread with some of jam. Place peach halves at

Apple-Stuffed Ham

Glazed Smoked Butt with Vegetables

one end of broiler rack, cut side down; place apple rings at other end; spread apple rings with jam. Return all to broiler; broil 5 minutes.

6. Meanwhile, peel bananas; halve crosswise; dip in lemon juice. Now turn peaches and brush with melted butter. Fit bananas here and there on rack and brush them with melted butter. Broil 5 minutes, or until bananas and peaches are golden.

7. Transfer ham slice to center of heated platter; spoon limas around it. On limas arrange broiled apple rings, peach halves, and bananas. Garnish with parsley. Makes 6 servings.

HAM STEAKS WITH GINGER SAUCE

1½ cups canned unsweet- ened pineapple juice	¾ cup fine gingersnap crumbs
½ cup vinegar	2 center-cut, ready-to-eat
¼ cup salad oil	ham slices, each 1 inch
⅓ cup liquid honey	thick

Early on day:
In saucepan combine pineapple juice, vinegar, salad oil, and honey; heat. Then stir in gingersnap crumbs; cover with wax paper; refrigerate until needed.

About 20 minutes before serving:
1. Preheat broiler 10 minutes, or as manufacturer directs. Reheat ginger sauce.
2. Meanwhile, with kitchen scissors or paring knife, cut fat edge of ham slices into diamond pattern. Place steaks on broiler rack, in broiler pan; brush with some of ginger sauce.
3. Broil, 3 inches from heat, 10 minutes, brushing on ginger sauce as needed. Turn steaks; broil 10 minutes longer.
4. Serve steaks, passing extra sauce. Makes 8 to 10 servings.

GLAZED SMOKED BUTT WITH VEGETABLES
(Pictured on page 25)

1 3-pound smoked boneless butt	Salt Brown sugar
Boiling water	Ginger ale
1 clove garlic	¼ teaspoon pepper
Whole cloves	¼ teaspoon dried whole
1 bay leaf	thyme
4 whole peppercorns	2 tablespoons butter or
8 medium carrots	margarine
8 medium parsnips	½ cup dark corn syrup

About 2 hours and 30 minutes before serving:
1. Place smoked butt in deep kettle; add boiling water to cover. Add garlic, 6 whole cloves, bay leaf, and peppercorns. Simmer, covered, about 1 hour and 30 minutes, or until fork-tender.

2. Meanwhile, wash and pare carrots and parsnips then cut each lengthwise into 3 or 4 long, diagonal wedges, halving any thick portions lengthwise. Cook in 1 quart boiling water with 1 tablespoon salt until just fork-tender.
3. Start heating oven to 400°F.
4. Make a series of diagonal slashes, about ⅛ inch deep and 1 inch apart, across top of smoked butt, forming diamonds. Stud top with whole cloves as pictured. Now pat a thick layer of brown sugar over top of butt, then place it on rack in small, shallow roasting pan.
5. Bake 20 minutes, basting with ginger ale two or three times.
6. Meanwhile, drain vegetables; toss with ¼ teaspoon salt, pepper, and thyme. Place in shallow 1½-quart casserole; dot with butter; pour on corn syrup. Bake with butt, basting often with syrup.
7. When meat is brown and glazed, and vegetables are shiny, remove from oven and arrange on platter as shown. Makes 6 servings.

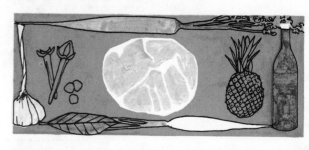

SMOKED BUTT, SOUTHERN STYLE

1 2- to 2½-pound boneless smoked shoulder butt	¼ cup vinegar 1 teaspoon dry mustard
Boiling water	2 1-pound 1-ounce cans
¼ cup butter or margarine	kidney beans, drained
½ cup minced onion	1 1-pound can green lima
1 clove garlic, minced	beans, drained
2 teaspoons brown sugar	½ cup catchup

About 3 hours before serving:
Place smoked butt in large kettle; add boiling water to cover. Simmer, covered, 2 hours, or until tender; drain.

About 15 minutes before butt is done:
1. Start heating oven to 350°F.
2. In hot butter, in skillet, sauté onion and garlic about 5 minutes, or until tender. Add brown sugar, vinegar, mustard, kidney and lima beans, and catchup; mix well. Taste, then add salt and pepper, if needed. Pour bean mixture into 2-quart casserole.
3. Cut smoked butt into slices ¾ inch thick; arrange meat slices over beans in casserole.
4. Bake, covered, about 15 minutes; then, uncover and bake 15 minutes longer. Makes 6 servings.

Lamb

LAMB CHOPS HARBERT

4 loin lamb chops, each 2 inches thick	1 clove garlic, cut
¼ pound Roquefort cheese	Salt
1 teaspoon Worcestershire	Pepper
Few drops Tabasco	Monosodium glutamate

In broiler:
1. Preheat broiler 10 minutes, or as manufacturer directs. Trim lamb chops of any excess fat.
2. Blend cheese, Worcestershire, and Tabasco. Rub each chop with garlic, then sprinkle with salt, pepper, and monosodium glutamate.
3. Broil chops, 3 inches from heat, 10 minutes on each side for medium-done; 12 to 14 minutes on each side for well-done. About 5 minutes before they are done, spread each chop with 2 tablespoons cheese mixture, then complete broiling. Makes 2 to 4 servings.

Or in oven:
1. Start heating oven to 350°F. Trim chops of any excess fat.
2. Follow step 2, above; then coat chops with cheese mixture. Stand on bone ends in 10-by-6-by-2-inch baking dish. Pour ½ can condensed consommé, undiluted, into dish.
3. Bake chops 45 minutes for medium-done; 1 hour and 15 minutes for well-done, basting occasionally with consommé in baking dish. Makes 2 to 4 servings.

GRILLED LAMB STEAKS
(Pictured on page 28)

1 or 2 cloves garlic, mashed or minced	¼ teaspoon pepper
⅓ cup salad oil	4 lamb steaks, each 1 inch thick
3 tablespoons soy sauce	1 1-pound 4½-ounce can sliced pineapple
2 tablespoons catchup	
1 tablespoon vinegar	

Night before, or at least 3 hours before serving:
Combine garlic, salad oil, soy sauce, catchup, vinegar, and pepper. Dip each steak in this mixture, coating well. Then let steaks stand in this marinade at least 3 hours, or overnight, if possible, turning a few times.
About 30 minutes before serving:
1. Preheat broiler 10 minutes, or as manufacturer directs.
2. Meanwhile, drain pineapple slices, then dry well on paper towels.

3. Lift lamb steaks from marinade to broiler pan; arrange pineapple slices around them.
4. Broil, 3 inches from heat, until brown—about 7 minutes, brushing occasionally with marinade. Then turn and broil about 7 minutes on other side, brushing with marinade occasionally.
5. Serve steaks with pineapple slices. Nice with tender-crisp small zucchini, halved lengthwise. Makes 4 servings.

LAMB WITH A GARLAND

1 leg of lamb, about 8 pounds	¼ cup butter or margarine
1 bunch radishes	½ teaspoon salt
1 6-ounce can frozen orange-juice concentrate	2 teaspoons canned, toasted slivered almonds
¼ cup lemon juice	1 bunch water cress

About 3 hours before serving:
1. Start heating oven to 325°F.
2. Place lamb, fat side up, on rack in shallow, open roasting pan. Insert roast-meat thermometer.
3. Roast 1 hour.
4. Meanwhile, cut stems from radishes, wash them, then pare off all red. With small, sharp knife make radish "snowdrops" as you would for radish roses, placing them in bowl of cold water.
5. In small saucepan combine orange-juice concentrate, lemon juice, butter, and salt; boil 5 minutes. Brush lamb with this mixture, then continue to roast 1½ to 2 hours longer, or until meat thermometer registers 170°F., brushing with orange-juice mixture occasionally. (If lamb becomes too brown, cover with foil.) About 15 minutes before lamb is done, sprinkle with almonds and brush with juice again.
6. When done, transfer lamb to heated platter; surround with water cress. Dot water-cress garland with radish "snowdrops," attaching a few to lamb with toothpicks. Serve with remaining orange-juice sauce in small pitcher. Makes about 8 servings, with leftovers.

ROAST LEG OF LAMB PIQUANT
(Pictured on page 28)

1 4-pound center-cut leg of lamb, trimmed weight	2 cloves garlic, finely minced
1 clove garlic, cut	¾ teaspoon salt
5 medium potatoes	Piquant Pickle Sauce, page 28
2 tablespoons salad oil	Snipped parsley

About 3 hours before serving:
1. Start heating oven to 325°F.
2. Meanwhile, remove the fell, that thin paperlike covering on the lamb. Do not wash meat; wipe with damp cloth. Rub lamb with cut clove of garlic. Place,

with fat side up, on rack in shallow open pan. Insert roast-meat thermometer through fat side into center of roast, so that it does not touch bone. Don't add water; don't cover.

3. Roast lamb 2½ to 3 hours, or until meat thermometer registers 175°F. — medium done. Don't baste or turn meat during roasting.

About 1 hour and 30 minutes before lamb is done:

1. Wash and pare potatoes; then cut each lengthwise into 6 wedges. Arrange potato wedges on cookie sheet covered with foil; turn up edges of foil all around. Sprinkle potatoes with salad oil, minced garlic, and salt. Then bake in same oven with lamb 1 hour, stirring occasionally with fork.

2. Meanwhile, make Piquant Pickle Sauce; keep hot.

3. When lamb is done, remove it to a heated platter. Place cookie sheet of potatoes under broiler for a few minutes to brown them.

4. Spoon Piquant Pickle Sauce over lamb; surround with potatoes; sprinkle with parsley. Serve with tender-crisp Brussels sprouts tossed with peas. Makes 4 servings.

PIQUANT PICKLE SAUCE: Melt ¼ cup butter or margarine; add 4½ teaspoons lemon or dill-pickle juice, ⅛ teaspoon cayenne pepper, 1 tablespoon snipped parsley (optional), and 2 tablespoons chopped dill pickle. Serve hot over lamb. (Nice on fish or cauliflower, too.)

RAGOUT OF LAMB
(Pictured here)

½ pound large dried lima beans	¼ teaspoon caraway seeds
1½ quarts cold water	2½ teaspoons salt
1½ pounds meat from lamb shanks	⅛ teaspoon pepper
	1 tablespoon regular all-purpose flour
2 tablespoons salad oil	½ pound medium carrots
3 cloves garlic, minced	½ pound small white onions
½ teaspoon dried basil	1 tablespoon snipped parsley
½ teaspoon dried rosemary	
1 bay leaf, crumbled	

Night before:

Place lima beans in large bowl; add water; let soak in refrigerator overnight.

About 2 hours and 30 minutes before serving:

1. Drain limas, reserving liquid. Trim any excess fat from meat; cut meat into 1½-inch chunks.

2. In Dutch oven heat salad oil; add lamb and garlic; brown lamb on all sides. Add basil, rosemary, bay leaf, caraway seeds, salt, pepper, and flour; toss together.

3. Add 3 cups reserved liquid and bring to boil. Add limas, bring to boil again; simmer, covered, 50 minutes, stirring occasionally.

4. Meanwhile, wash, scrape, then cut carrots into diagonal pieces, 1½ to 2 inches thick. Peel and wash

Grilled Lamb Steaks, Ragout of Lamb, Roast Leg of Lamb Piquant

onions; add carrots and onions to meat mixture; bring to boil; simmer, covered, 30 minutes, or until vegetables are tender.

5. Arrange ragout in warm serving dish; sprinkle with snipped parsley and serve piping hot. Makes about 4 servings.

INDIVIDUAL LAMB ROASTS

1 clove garlic, quartered	¼ cup lemon juice
4 lamb shanks, well trimmed of fat	2 bay leaves
	4 whole peppercorns
¼ cup regular all-purpose flour	4 medium sweet potatoes, pared, halved
Salt	1 9-ounce package frozen cut green beans, thawed just enough to separate
1 teaspoon paprika	
2 tablespoons salad oil	

About 2 hours and 30 minutes before serving:

1. Insert piece of garlic into each lamb shank. On wax paper combine flour, 2 teaspoons salt, and paprika; roll lamb shanks in this mixture until they are well coated.
2. Start heating oven to 350°F.
3. In hot salad oil, in skillet, brown lamb shanks well on all sides; place in 3-quart casserole. Add lemon juice to oil in skillet; stir to loosen browned bits; pour over lamb shanks. Add bay leaves and peppercorns.
4. Bake lamb shanks, covered, 1 hour. Then top with sweet potatoes and thawed beans; sprinkle with 1 teaspoon salt. Bake, covered, 1 hour longer, or until meat is fork-tender. Makes 4 servings.

GARDEN STATE LAMB STEW

⅓ cup regular all-purpose flour	2 1-pound cans tomatoes
Salt	1 teaspoon paprika
½ teaspoon pepper	Several dashes Tabasco
4 pounds lamb neck, cut into cubes with bone in	6 medium carrots
	6 medium potatoes
3 tablespoons salad oil	8 small white onions

About 1 hour and 45 minutes before serving:

1. In medium bowl combine flour, 1 teaspoon salt, and pepper; use to coat each lamb piece well.
2. In hot salad oil, in large Dutch oven, sauté lamb pieces until well browned. Pour on tomatoes; add paprika, 2 teaspoons salt, and Tabasco. Simmer, covered, 30 minutes.
3. Meanwhile, pare and quarter carrots. Pare potatoes. Add carrots and potatoes to stew; simmer, covered, about 20 minutes.
4. Now stir stew; add peeled onions; cover and simmer about 30 minutes, or until meat and vegetables are fork-tender. Skim fat off surface, if desired. Makes 6 servings.

Veal

Veal is a meat much honored in Europe, but too often neglected in America. This should not be, for veal when adequately seasoned and properly cooked, is one of the most flavorsome of all meats—and pound for-pound it is a good meat buy because there is practically no waste. Because there is so little fat, veal is best roasted, braised, or cooked in liquid.

STUFFED VEAL POT ROAST

6 white bread slices, in ½-inch cubes	¼ teaspoon garlic salt
1 tablespoon snipped parsley	1⅓ cups canned chicken broth
1 small onion, minced	1 3-pound boned breast of veal
1 3- or 4-ounce can sliced mushrooms, drained	¼ teaspoon pepper
	Paprika
1 large carrot, finely grated	2 tablespoons shortening
1 small parsnip, finely grated	1 cup white wine
	6 medium potatoes
1 large stalk celery, finely chopped	6 to 8 canned whole un-peeled apricots, drained
2 eggs, beaten	¼ cup light cream (optional)
Salt	

About 2 hours and 30 minutes before serving:

1. In large bowl combine bread, parsley, onion, mushrooms, carrot, parsnip, celery, eggs, ¾ teaspoon salt, and garlic salt; moisten with ⅓ cup chicken broth.
2. Lay veal out flat and sprinkle with 1 teaspoon salt, and pepper; spread mushroom-carrot mixture on veal; roll up, jelly-roll fashion, tie securely with string. Rub meat roll with paprika.
3. In hot shortening, in Dutch oven, brown veal roll on all sides, then add wine and 1 cup chicken broth; simmer about 1 hour.
4. Meanwhile, pare potatoes; lay in Dutch oven around roast; sprinkle each with salt. Simmer 1 hour longer, or until potatoes are done and veal is tender. Remove roast and potatoes to heated platter; keep warm.
5. Meanwhile, in Dutch oven place apricots; heat 5 minutes, or until hot. Now remove string from roast; arrange hot apricots around meat and potatoes on platter. Heat drippings in Dutch oven; add light cream, strain, then pass with meat. Makes 6 servings.

VEAL WITH LEMON JUICE

3 pounds boned veal shoulder, in one piece	3 tablespoons butter or margarine
1¼ teaspoons salt	1 tablespoon regular all-purpose flour
¼ teaspoon pepper	
Lemon juice	

About 2 hours and 30 minutes before serving:

1. Rub veal with salt, pepper, and 2 tablespoons lemon juice.
2. In Dutch oven melt butter; in it brown veal; then add ⅓ cup lemon juice and ⅔ cup water. Simmer, covered, 2 hours, or until tender.
3. Slice veal. Skim fat from gravy; mix flour with a little water; stir into gravy; then cook until thickened. Spoon some of gravy over meat slices; pass rest. Makes 6 servings.

LOUISIANA BAYOU POTTED VEAL

½ cup regular all-purpose flour	2 tablespoons salad oil or shortening
1 teaspoon seasoned salt	1 1-pound can tomatoes
⅛ teaspoon pepper	1 teaspoon monosodium glutamate
½ teaspoon sage	
1 6-pound rolled boned veal shoulder	

1. Combine flour, seasoned salt, pepper, and sage; use to coat veal thoroughly. Reserve any leftover flour.
2. In hot salad oil, in Dutch oven, brown veal well on all sides—about 15 to 20 minutes. Add 2 tablespoons water; simmer, covered, 2 hours, adding more water, if necessary. Then add tomatoes and monosodium glutamate; simmer, covered, 1 hour, or until veal is fork-tender.
3. Lift veal to heated platter. Skim fat from liquid in Dutch oven; place fat in small bowl. To fat, add reserved flour; blend well; stir into liquid in Dutch oven. Cook, stirring constantly, until thickened. Strain, if desired; pass separately. Makes 10 servings.

OVEN-SPECIAL VEAL

1 3-pound veal steak, ½ inch thick	½ teaspoon basil
3 cups bite-size shredded corn cereal	¼ teaspoon thyme
	¼ cup milk
¼ cup regular all-purpose flour	Seasoned salt
	¼ cup bacon fat
¾ teaspoon salt	1 medium onion, sliced
½ teaspoon celery salt	½ cup dry white wine

1. Start heating oven to 350°F.
2. Cut veal steak into 6 serving-size pieces.
3. Crush cereal, making 1⅓ cups crumbs; stir in flour, salt, celery salt, basil, and thyme.

4. Dip veal in milk; sprinkle with seasoned salt, then dip in crumbs.
5. In hot bacon fat, in skillet, brown veal on both sides. Transfer veal to 13-by-9-by-2-inch baking dish. Lay onion slice on each piece; then pour on wine.
6. Bake, covered with foil, 45 minutes; uncover and bake 20 minutes longer, or until slightly crisp. Makes 6 servings.

VEAL, ROMAN STYLE

2 pounds very thin veal cutlets (12)	12 paper-thin slices prosciutto or cooked ham
¼ teaspoon pepper	¼ cup butter or margarine
1 teaspoon powdered sage	¼ cup white wine
	Hot fluffy rice

About 1 hour before serving:

1. Using edge of heavy saucer, pound cutlets well. Sprinkle both sides with pepper and sage. On each piece of veal lay a slice of prosciutto; roll up, secure with toothpicks.
2. In hot butter, in large skillet, sauté veal rolls until well browned. Add wine; simmer, covered, about 30 minutes, or until fork-tender, adding about ¼ cup water to sauce in skillet, if necessary. Remove toothpicks.
3. Serve over hot fluffy rice. Makes 6 to 8 servings.

HUNGARIAN VEAL ROLLS

8 thin veal-cutlet slices, put through cuber	1 slice red onion
	1 tablespoon butter or margarine
1 teaspoon salt	1 beef-bouillon cube
½ teaspoon pepper	1 teaspoon cornstarch
Seasoned salt	1 cup commercial sour cream
3 slices bacon	
2 dill pickles, quartered lengthwise	Snipped parsley

About 1 hour and 30 minutes before serving:

1. Season one side of each veal slice with salt, pepper, and a sprinkle of seasoned salt. Then, crosswise, in center of each veal slice place ⅓ slice bacon, one quarter of pickle, and few strips of red-onion slice. Roll up each veal slice; secure with toothpick.

Veal Steaks à la Zingara

2. In large skillet, sauté remaining bit of bacon until fat cooks out. Remove bacon; to bacon fat add butter; in this sauté veal rolls until brown on all sides. Add bouillon cube and 1 cup water; simmer, covered, 1 hour, turning rolls at end of ½ hour. Transfer veal rolls to heated platter; remove picks.

3. Make a paste of cornstarch and 2 tablespoons water; stir into gravy in skillet. Cook over medium heat until thickened; then remove from heat and pour some of it into sour cream, then stir sour cream back into gravy until thoroughly mixed. Pour gravy over veal rolls, garnish with parsley. Makes 4 servings.

VEAL À LA SUISSE

6 thin veal cutlets (about 1½ pounds)	1 cup sauterne or white wine
6 thin slices natural Swiss cheese	1 10½-ounce can beef gravy
6 paper-thin slices cooked ham	½ cup light cream
2 tablespoons regular all-purpose flour	Dash salt
½ teaspoon paprika	About 4 cups hot fluffy rice
⅓ cup butter or margarine	Snipped parsley

1. Using edge of heavy saucer, pound each veal cutlet well; then cut each in half. On each of 6 cutlet halves place ½ cheese slice; then 1 ham slice, folded over; then another ½ cheese slice. Cover each with a second veal cutlet half; fasten securely with toothpicks or poultry pins. Now coat cutlets on both sides with flour-paprika mixture.

2. In hot butter, in skillet, brown cutlets on both sides. Add ½ cup wine; simmer, uncovered, until liquid is almost completely absorbed. Add ½ cup wine, gravy, cream, and salt; simmer, covered, 10 minutes, or until fork-tender.

3. Just before serving, remove toothpicks. Arrange cutlets on hot fluffy rice; sprinkle with parsley. Makes 6 servings.

VEAL STEAKS À LA ZINGARA
(Pictured opposite)

8 medium veal slices, ¼ to ½ inch thick (about 2¼ pounds)	1 tablespoon cornstarch
2 teaspoons seasoned salt	1 cup cold water
	¾ cup milk or cream
3 tablespoons butter or margarine	Creamy Scallion Potatoes, below
8 medium fresh or canned mushroom caps	8 bacon slices
	2 white bread slices
	¼ cup Madeira
	1 tomato, in 8 wedges

About 45 minutes before serving:

1. Shape each veal slice into a circle by joining two ends, then fastening with toothpicks. Sprinkle all over with seasoned salt.

2. In large skillet, in hot butter, sauté veal slices until browned, turning once; add mushroom caps and sauté them until golden. Remove from heat.

3. In small bowl stir cornstarch with water and milk until smooth. Pour over veal slices and mushrooms in skillet. Simmer, covered, about 15 minutes, or until meat is tender.

4. Meanwhile make Creamy Scallion Potatoes. Sauté bacon until lightly browned and curly. Toast bread slices lightly, then quarter them.

5. When meat is tender, pour on Madeira; bring to boil; remove from heat. Remove picks from meat.

6. In center of large serving platter pile potatoes, with toast on both sides. On each piece of toast place one veal slice, then top with a mushroom cap. Pour some of gravy around meat; pass rest. Garnish with bacon strips and tomato wedges. Makes about 6 servings.

CREAMY SCALLION POTATOES: Ten minutes before serving, prepare 1 8-serving package instant mashed potatoes as label directs. Blend in 4 scallions, cut into ¾-inch slices; pile on serving platter.

SAVORY VEAL STEW

6 bacon slices	1 teaspoon salt
1 3-pound shoulder of veal, cut into 1½-inch cubes	⅛ teaspoon thyme
	⅛ teaspoon crushed rosemary leaves
3 large onions, sliced	2 tablespoons butter or margarine
2 cloves garlic	
½ teaspoon curry powder	½ pound fresh mushrooms, sliced
1½ cups boiling water	⅓ cup sherry
1 10½-ounce can condensed tomato soup, undiluted	½ cup snipped parsley

About 2 hours before serving:

1. In Dutch oven fry bacon slices until crisp; drain on paper towels; crumble and set aside.

2. From Dutch oven remove all but 3 tablespoons bacon fat. In this, lightly brown veal cubes on all sides; add onions and garlic; continue cooking, stirring, until veal is well-browned. Add curry powder and boiling water; stir to scrape up brown bits from bottom and sides of Dutch oven.

3. Now add crumbled bacon, soup, salt, thyme, and rosemary; blend thoroughly. Simmer, covered, over low heat, 1 hour.

4. About 10 minutes before hour is up, in medium skillet melt butter; in it sauté mushrooms about 5 minutes. Stir into stew with sherry. Remove garlic; then sprinkle stew with parsley.

5. Serve over hot rice or noodles, or with baked or mashed potatoes. Makes 8 servings.

Variety Meats

MUSHROOM-AND-KIDNEY SAUTÉ

3 tablespoons butter or
  margarine
½ green pepper, minced
2 medium onions, minced
4 veal kidneys
4½ teaspoons regular
  all-purpose flour

½ pound fresh mushrooms,
  sliced
1¼ teaspoons salt
Speck pepper
2 tablespoons water
2 tablespoons sherry

1. In hot butter, in skillet, sauté green pepper and onions until tender.
2. Meanwhile, cut membranes from kidneys; cube, then sprinkle kidneys with flour. Add kidneys and mushrooms to onions; sprinkle with salt and pepper.
3. When kidneys are lightly browned, simmer them, uncovered, 10 minutes. Add water; cook until thickened; add sherry.
4. Serve kidneys on fluffy rice. Makes 6 servings.

STEAK AND KIDNEY PIE

Piecrust for 1 crust
4 small veal kidneys
Salt
1 cup Burgundy
1½ pounds round steak
Seasoned instant meat
  tenderizer
½ cup unsifted regular
  all-purpose flour
½ teaspoon pepper

¼ cup salad oil
½ cup frozen chopped
  onion
1 bay leaf
¼ cup snipped parsley
¼ cup snipped celery tops
½ teaspoon marjoram
¼ pound fresh mushrooms,
  sliced
1 egg yolk, slightly beaten

About 2 hours before serving:
1. Prepare piecrust for 1 crust from package mix or favorite recipe; wrap in wax paper; refrigerate.
2. Trim fat and remove membrane from kidneys; then cut kidneys into small clusters. Sprinkle lightly with about 1 teaspoon salt; place in small bowl; cover with Burgundy; set aside.
3. Cut round steak, across grain, into thin strips, removing fat. Treat with meat tenderizer as label directs, then coat with mixture of flour, 1 teaspoon salt, and pepper, reserving any leftover flour. In hot oil, in Dutch oven, sauté onion until golden; add steak strips; sauté until brown.
4. Remove kidneys from Burgundy, reserving Burgundy. Dust kidneys lightly with reserved flour mixture; add to steak strips in Dutch oven and cook, stirring carefully, until browned. Add ½ cup water, bay leaf,

parsley, celery tops, and marjoram. Simmer, covered, over low heat, about 1 hour, or until steak strips are fork-tender.
5. Start heating oven to 450°F.
6. Into meats stir mushrooms and reserved Burgundy; pour into 1½-quart casserole. Roll out piecrust; lay over top of casserole, sealing edges as for pie; make 3 or 4 slashes in top; brush with egg yolk. Set casserole on foil in oven.
7. Bake 20 to 25 minutes, or until golden. Makes 4 to 6 servings.

FOUR-IN-ONE KIDNEY BAKE

6 medium onions
½ cup water
Butter or margarine
Salt
Pepper
6 medium baking potatoes,
  scrubbed

12 lamb kidneys, split
  crosswise, fat removed
8 bacon slices
6 medium tomatoes
Few buttered fresh bread
  crumbs

1. Start heating oven to 400°F.
2. At one end of 12-by-8-by-2-inch baking dish, group onions; add water; dot with butter; sprinkle with salt and pepper; cover with foil.
3. Bake onions, along with potatoes, 45 minutes.
4. Meanwhile, soak kidneys in warm, salted water 15 minutes; drain. Arrange in shallow baking dish; sprinkle with salt and pepper; crisscross top with 2 bacon strips. Remove small slice from top of each tomato; season with salt and pepper; arrange, uncovered, at end of baking dish containing onions. Reduce oven temperature to 325°F.
5. Bake kidneys, onions, and tomatoes 30 minutes longer.
6. Meanwhile, in skillet, cook rest of bacon until crisp; roll into curls; keep warm.
Just before serving:
1. Fix baked potatoes ready for eating; transfer to serving dish.
2. Top onions and tomatoes with crumbs; run under broiler to brown.

3. Arrange kidneys in center of wooden board or large heated platter; garnish with bacon curls. Arrange onions and tomatoes alternately around kidneys. Makes 6 servings.

LIVER POT ROAST IMPERIAL

1 2½- to 3-pound calf liver, unsliced	1 cup canned bouillon or consommé, undiluted
3 salt-pork slices, ¼ inch thick	1 large onion, sliced
¼ cup brandy	6 bacon slices, diced
¼ cup snipped parsley	12 small whole white onions
⅓ cup olive or salad oil	½ cup white wine
2 bay leaves	2 to 3 teaspoons granulated sugar
2 tablespoons lemon juice	
½ cup butter or margarine	½ cup light cream
1 teaspoon salt	2 egg yolks, well beaten
¼ teaspoon pepper	

1. In large bowl place liver, salt-pork slices, brandy, parsley, oil, bay leaves, and lemon juice; refrigerate 15 minutes. Turn liver; refrigerate 15 minutes longer. Drain liver, reserving salt pork and liquid (marinade).
2. In hot butter, in Dutch oven, brown liver well on all sides, using wooden spoons to turn it. Add salt, pepper, ½ cup bouillon, and marinade; on top of liver place salt-pork and onion slices. Simmer, covered, 1 hour, basting occasionally and turning once or twice (replace salt pork on top of liver each time).
3. Meanwhile, in hot skillet, cook bacon until crisp and golden; set aside. Pour off all but 2 tablespoons bacon fat; in same skillet brown whole onions; add ½ cup bouillon; simmer, covered, about 20 minutes, or until onions are tender. Remove liver and onions to heated platter.
4. Into combined pan juices stir wine, sugar, and cream; heat slowly. Carefully stir in egg yolks; cook until thickened; strain.
5. Slice liver; sprinkle with bacon bits. Pass sauce separately. Nice served with French fries. Makes 6 to 8 servings.

VENETIAN LIVER

¼ cup butter or margarine	1 tablespoon regular all-purpose flour
2 medium onions, minced	
1 pound thin beef or calf liver, cut into very narrow strips	1½ teaspoons salt
	¼ teaspoon pepper
	½ cup dry white wine

About 10 minutes before serving:
1. In hot butter, in skillet, sauté onions until golden; stir in liver, flour, salt, and pepper; blend until liver loses red color.
2. Add wine and ¼ cup water; heat. Serve over hot fluffy rice. Makes 4 servings.

OXJOINT AND BARLEY STEW

2 oxtails, cut into 2-inch joints	1 1-pound 3-ounce can tomatoes
¼ cup regular all-purpose flour	Boiling water
	5 teaspoons salt
1 tablespoon shortening	1 teaspoon sugar
1 clove garlic, minced	½ teaspoon pepper
6 medium onions, sliced	½ cup pearl barley
1 green pepper, minced	6 carrots, quartered

About 3 hours before serving:
1. Roll oxjoints in flour; in hot shortening, in Dutch oven, brown oxjoints. Remove them; in same Dutch oven, sauté garlic and onions until golden.
2. Return oxjoints to Dutch oven; add green pepper, tomatoes, 1 tomato can of boiling water, salt, sugar, and pepper. Bring to boil; add barley. Simmer, covered, 1½ hours, stirring occasionally.
3. Add carrots; cook 1 hour, or until carrots are tender, skim off fat if necessary. Makes 6 servings.

GRILLED OXJOINTS BORDELAISE

3 oxjoints, cut in sections	3 tablespoons melted butter or margarine
1½ teaspoons mixed pickling spice	
1 bay leaf	3 tablespoons prepared mustard
2 onions, sliced	½ cup packaged dried bread crumbs
2 small carrots, sliced	
1½ cups cut-up celery	Sliced radishes
2½ teaspoons salt	Bordelaise Sauce, below
¼ teaspoon pepper	(optional)

About 3 hours and 30 minutes before serving:
1. Place oxjoints in Dutch oven; add boiling water to barely cover. Add pickling spice, bay leaf, onions, carrots, celery, salt, and pepper; simmer, covered, 2½ to 3 hours. Remove oxjoints to broiler rack. Refrigerate broth (next day skim, then heat for soup).
2. Preheat broiler 10 minutes, or as manufacturer directs.
3. Combine melted butter and mustard; brush half over top of oxjoints. Sprinkle half of bread crumbs over oxjoints. Then turn them, brush with rest of mustard-butter, and sprinkle with rest of crumbs.
4. Broil oxjoints until golden brown on one side, then turn them and broil on other side.
5. Heap oxjoints on heated platter; garnish with radishes. Pass Bordelaise Sauce. Makes 6 to 8 servings.

BORDELAISE SAUCE: Early on day, in 2 tablespoons hot butter or margarine, in skillet, sauté 1 shallot, minced, 1 onion slice, 2 carrot slices, parsley sprig, 6 whole peppercorns, 1 whole clove, and ½ bay leaf until onion is golden and tender. Add 2 tablespoons regular all-purpose flour; cook over low heat, stirring, until flour is lightly browned. Stir in 1 10½-ounce can beef bouillon, undiluted; simmer, stirring, until thickened and smooth—about 10 minutes; strain. Add ¼ teaspoon salt, ⅛ teaspoon pepper, ¼ cup dry red wine, and 1 tablespoon snipped parsley; refrigerate. About 15 minutes before serving, reheat sauce, covered, in double broiler (if too thick, add 1 or 2 tablespoons wine). Spoon sauce over oxjoints; pass rest.

SMOKED TONGUE, PORTUGUESE

1 3-pound smoked tongue	1 bay leaf
1½ tablespoons butter or margarine	¼ teaspoon cumin or caraway seeds
1 large onion, sliced	1 tablespoon vinegar or white wine
½ cup canned tomatoes	
1½ teaspoons salt	2 cups hot cooked sliced carrots
¼ teaspoon pepper	
½ teaspoon celery salt	8 hot cooked parslied potatoes
2 whole cloves	

About 3 hours before serving:
1.   Place tongue in Dutch oven; cover with hot water; simmer about 2½ hours, or until tender. Skin tongue, then slice.
2.   Pour stock from Dutch oven; then in butter, in same Dutch oven, brown onions. Add tomatoes; cook 5 minutes. Then add salt, pepper, celery salt, cloves, bay leaf, cumin, and vinegar.
3.   Lay tongue in sauce; simmer, covered, about 10 minutes, or until very tender. Arrange on platter, with carrots and potatoes around it. Makes 6 servings.

CUMBERLAND TONGUE PLATTER
(Pictured below)

1 smoked beef tongue (about 4 pounds)	2 tablespoons prepared mustard
Glazed Sweets, page 37	1 tablespoon lemon juice
Quick-Cooked Zucchini, page 37	1 tablespoon slivered orange peel
1 cup currant jelly	

About 4 hours before serving:
1.   Wash tongue well; place in large kettle or Dutch oven; cover with cold water. Simmer, covered, about 3 to 3½ hours, or until fork-tender; remove from stock; cool slightly.
2.   About 1½ hours before tongue is done, start Glazed Sweets as directed.
3.   When tongue is tender, trim it of bone and gristle; then, with help of paring knife, peel off skin. Cut tongue into long, thin slices.
About 25 minutes before serving:
1.   Start Quick-Cooked Zucchini as directed.
2.   In skillet, over medium heat, melt jelly with mustard and lemon juice; stir until blended and smooth. Add orange peel. Now add tongue slices, one at a time, making sure each slice is coated with sauce. Cover and

Cumberland Tongue Platter

heat slowly 10 to 15 minutes, or until thoroughly hot.

3. Arrange folded tongue slices down center of large heated platter, with sweets and zucchini on either side. Pass extra sauce. Makes 8 servings.

GLAZED SWEETS: About 1½ hours before serving, start heating oven to 375°F. Place 6 unpared medium sweet potatoes in large saucepan; cover with boiling water; add 1 teaspoon salt. Simmer, covered, 15 minutes. Drain potatoes, peel, and halve lengthwise. Arrange in 2-quart casserole. In small saucepan, over medium heat, melt ¼ cup butter or margarine. Add ½ teaspoon nutmeg, ⅛ teaspoon pepper, 1½ teaspoons salt, and 1 cup dark corn syrup. Stir until blended; pour over potatoes. Bake, covered, about 1 hour, or until tender and glazed, basting frequently.

QUICK-COOKED ZUCCHINI: About 25 minutes before serving, in medium saucepan, melt 2 tablespoons butter or margarine. Add 2 medium onions, thinly sliced, then sauté until golden. Add 2 pounds washed zucchini, sliced diagonally ¼ inch thick, 2 teaspoons salt, ⅛ teaspoon pepper, and 1 cup boiling water. Simmer, covered, about 10 minutes, or until zucchini is fork-tender; drain. Season to taste with seasoned salt.

SWEETBREADS EN BROCHETTE

½ pound veal sweetbreads	⅛ teaspoon pepper
Salt	6 bacon slices, halved
Lemon juice	¼ cup melted butter or
12 small mushrooms	margarine
1 teaspoon Worcestershire	Snipped parsley

Day before:

1. Simmer sweetbreads 20 minutes in water to cover, adding 1 teaspoon salt and 1 tablespoon lemon juice for each quart of water used. (The acid helps to keep the sweetbreads white and firm.)

2. Then, holding sweetbreads under cold running water, slip off membrane with fingers. With knife, cut out dark veins and thick connective tissue. Cut sweetbreads into 12 chunks; refrigerate, covered.

3. Remove stems from mushrooms; place mushroom caps in bowl. Combine 3 tablespoons lemon juice, Worcestershire, ½ teaspoon salt, and pepper; pour over mushroom caps; refrigerate, tossing occasionally.

About 30 minutes before serving:

1. Preheat broiler 10 minutes, or as manufacturer directs.

2. Roll up each bacon slice. On each of 3 10-inch skewers, string sweetbread chunks, mushrooms caps, then bacon rolls. Arrange, side-by-side, in shallow, open pan; brush with some of butter.

3. Broil, 6 inches from heat, 15 to 20 minutes, or until sweetbreads are golden and mushrooms done, turning often and brushing with butter. Pour on remaining butter; sprinkle with parsley. Makes 2 servings.

Canned and Ready-to-Eat Meats

SPEEDY "SQUARE" MEAL

2 12-ounce cans luncheon meat	1 tablespoon prepared mustard
18 whole cloves	½ cup apricot preserves
1 package refrigerated crescent rolls	Pickled watermelon slices

About 30 minutes before serving:

1. Start heating oven to 375°F.

2. Cut each can luncheon meat into 9 squares almost to bottom; stud each square with a clove. Arrange on ovenproof platter.

3. Cut crescent rolls into 8 or 9 *slices;* arrange around meat. Spread meat, including cuts and tops of rolls with mustard, then with apricot preserves.

4. Bake 20 minutes, or until rolls are golden. Garnish with pickled watermelon. Makes 4 to 6 servings.

LUNCHEON MEAT À LA HOLSTEIN

1 egg	Salad oil
½ cup sifted regular all-purpose flour	⅓ cup milk
½ teaspoon double-acting baking powder	1 12-ounce can luncheon meat

About 45 minutes before serving:

1. In bowl, with fork, beat egg; add flour sifted with baking powder, 1 teaspoon oil, and milk; beat until smooth.

2. In skillet heat salad oil, about ½ inch deep. Slice luncheon meat into 6 slices, crosswise; coat each slice with batter; fry until golden, turning once. Drain on paper towels. Nice with catchup. Makes 4 servings.

HAWAIIAN HASH

1 16-ounce can corned-beef hash	4 canned pineapple slices
	Catchup

1. Start heating oven to 400°F.

2. Remove both ends from can of hash; push hash out in one piece; cut into 4 slices.

3. Top each pineapple slice with hash slice, then with a bit of catchup. Wrap each in foil.

4. Bake 20 minutes; unwrap; serve at once. Makes 4 servings.

SPICY HASH

3 tablespoons butter or margarine	4 teaspoons green-pickle relish
1 medium onion, chopped	⅓ cup catchup
1 15-ounce can corned-beef hash	Dash Tabasco
	Snipped parsley

About 15 minutes before serving:

1. In melted butter, in skillet, sauté onion until golden; then stir in hash, relish, catchup, and Tabasco. Cook, stirring occasionally, 10 minutes.
2. Arrange hash on warm platter; sprinkle with parsley. Serve at once. Makes 4 servings.

STUFFED GREEN PEPPERS

2 large green peppers	½ teaspoon Worcestershire
1 1-pound can corned-beef hash	Pinch pepper
¼ cup catchup	½ 10¾-ounce can beef gravy
¼ teaspoon seasoned salt	

About 1 hour before serving:

1. Start heating oven to 375°F.
2. Seed green peppers, leaving them whole. Mix hash with catchup, seasoned salt, Worcestershire, and pepper. Use this mixture to fill peppers; arrange in 1-quart casserole; pour gravy over all.
3. Bake, covered, 45 minutes, or until peppers are fork-tender. Makes 2 servings.

BARBECUED BOLOGNA CROWN

¼ cup butter or margarine	1 1-pound fresh loaf Italian bread
½ cup minced onion	12 Bologna slices, ¼ inch thick, peeled
1 cup chili sauce	
¼ cup vinegar	½ cup grated process Cheddar cheese
2 tablespoons Worcestershire	1 1-pound 13-ounce can spiced apricots, well drained
4 teaspoons brown sugar	
1 teaspoon celery salt	
½ teaspoon prepared mustard	Scallions

About 30 minutes before serving:

1. Start heating oven to 400°F.
2. In hot butter, in saucepan, sauté onion until tender. Stir in chili sauce, vinegar, Worcestershire, brown sugar, celery salt, and mustard. Cook, uncovered, over low heat 5 minutes, or until thickened.
3. Meanwhile, cut bread into 13 crosswise slices, not quite through to bottom crust; place on large piece of foil on cookie sheet. Turn loaf on its side; into each cut insert 1 tablespoon chili-sauce mixture, then 1 Bologna slice, folded in half; loaf bends into crown shape as it is filled.
4. Spread remaining chili-sauce mixture over loaf;

sprinkle with grated cheese. Wrap loaf completely in foil.
5. Bake 15 minutes; now lift loaf, with wide spatulas, to serving platter. With kitchen scissors, cut away foil. Fill center with apricots and stand a few scallions upright among them.
6. To serve, snip slices apart with scissors; eat with knife and fork. Makes 6 servings of 2 slices each.

FRANKFURTER GOULASH
(Pictured opposite)

3 to 4 tablespoons butter or margarine	1 teaspoon basil
1 to 2 cloves garlic, minced	1 10½-ounce can condensed consommé, undiluted
2 medium onions, in ¼-inch slices	1¼ pounds zucchini, cut in 1-inch slices
8 frankfurters, each cut into 3 diagonal slices	1 8-serving package instant mashed potatoes
½ to 1 teaspoon chili powder	1 medium tomato, sliced
1 tablespoon regular all-purpose flour	Water cress
1 teaspoon seasoned salt	Instant minced onion (optional)

About 40 minutes before serving:

1. In hot butter, in large skillet, sauté garlic, onions, and frankfurters until golden. Stir in chili powder, flour, seasoned salt, basil, and consommé; over it lay zucchini. Bring to boil; then simmer, covered, about 20 minutes, or until zucchini is tender.
2. Meanwhile, make up mashed potatoes as package label directs. Heap goulash in center of large serving dish; tuck in tomato slices here and there. Place mashed potatoes in mounds around it; garnish with water cress; then, if desired, sprinkle potatoes lightly with instant minced onion. Makes 8 servings.

LIVERWURST AU GOURMET

1 cup uncooked regular or processed white rice	½ cup snipped parsley
1½ pounds liverwurst, unsliced	2 drops Tabasco
	1 medium onion, grated
½ cup very soft butter or margarine	1 tablespoon Worcestershire
	2 tablespoons sherry

1. Preheat broiler 10 minutes, or as manufacturer directs. Cook rice as package label directs.
2. Meanwhile, cut liverwurst on angle into 8 slices; place in shallow pan. In small bowl combine butter, parsley, Tabasco, onion, Worcestershire, and sherry. Spread on liverwurst.
3. Broil, 3 inches from heat, about 6 minutes, or until browned. Arrange bed of rice on heated platter; top with meat; spoon on pan juices. Makes 4 servings.

Frankfurter Goulash

BROILER-STYLE DINNER
(Pictured on page 16)

2 16-ounce cans whole
    white potatoes
½ cup melted butter or
    margarine
Paprika
Salt
1 1-pound can whole green
    beans, drained

Nutmeg
1 1-pound can cling-peach
    halves
Curry powder
5 frankfurters
Prepared mustard
1 tablespoon instant
    minced onion

About 30 minutes before serving:

1. Preheat broiler 10 minutes, or as manufacturer directs.

2. Drain potatoes well; arrange them on broiler rack. Brush potatoes with some of melted butter; dust with paprika; then sprinkle lightly with salt.

3. Broil, turning often, about 10 minutes; push to one side of broiler rack.

4. Meanwhile, toss beans with 2 tablespoons melted butter; season with salt and dash nutmeg; place on broiler rack.

5. Brush 5 well-drained peach halves with melted butter (refrigerate rest of peach halves for later use); sprinkle with curry powder; place on broiler rack.

6. Split frankfurters lengthwise, almost, but not quite through; brush with melted butter; spread cut side with mustard; place, cut side down, on broiler rack.

7. Broil all, about 4 inches from heat, about 7 minutes, or until franks are hot, turning once and sprinkling potatoes with minced onion; brush with melted butter as needed.

8. Serve right from broiler rack, or rearrange on heated platter. Makes 4 servings.

40

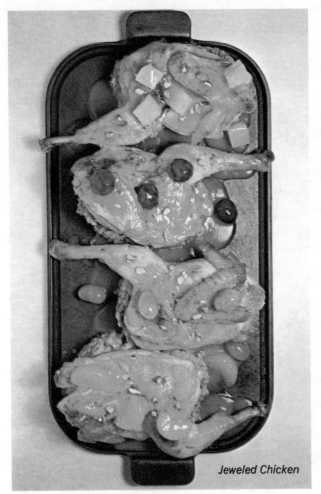

Jeweled Chicken

Drumstick Crown

Glazed Chicken Wings

Rotisserie Twins

Chicken Dishes

ROTISSERIE TWINS
(Pictured opposite)

2 2½-pound broiler-fryers	½ pound fresh mushrooms
Melted butter or margarine	2 medium tomatoes
1 tablespoon lemon juice	½ cup bottled herb-French dressing
Seasoned salt	2 12-ounce cans whole-kernel corn
Seasoned pepper	
Fresh parsley	1 cup light cream
Paprika	Bottled sauce for gravy

About 1 hour and 30 minutes before serving:

1. Brush inside neck and body cavities of chickens with mixture of 2 tablespoons melted butter and lemon juice; sprinkle each with ¼ teaspoon seasoned salt and ⅛ teaspoon seasoned pepper; stuff each with ½ cup parsley sprigs, packed.

2. On each chicken tie ends of legs together with string, tying around tail to hold body opening together. Then lift one of wings up and out, forcing tip back until it rests flat against neck skin; repeat with other wing.

3. Brush outside surfaces of each chicken with 1 tablespoon melted butter; rub in ¼ teaspoon seasoned salt and ⅛ teaspoon seasoned pepper, then sprinkle with paprika.

4. Put chickens on rotisserie spit, with breast side of one facing up, the other facing down. Skewer or tie them to spit so they are balanced and will rotate smoothly. Then roast, following rotisserie directions. Roasting time will be about 1 hour. When done, chickens should be nicely browned, crisp, and fleshy part of drumstick should be soft when pressed or pierced.

5. Meanwhile, cut 8 lengthwise slices, ¼ inch thick, from mushrooms; chop rest. Cut tomatoes into 8 slices, ½ inch thick; spread with French dressing; set aside.

6. In medium saucepan melt 2 tablespoons butter; in it sauté cleaned whole giblets and chopped mushrooms 10 minutes; then add 1 cup water, ¼ teaspoon seasoned salt, and dash seasoned pepper; simmer, covered, about 20 minutes, or until giblets are tender.

7. Heat corn in 2 tablespoons butter, then season as desired.

8. When done, chop giblets finely; return to gravy in saucepan. Add cream and enough bottled sauce for gravy to make a nice brown color; bring to boil, thin with water if necessary, then pour into gravy boat.

9. When chickens are done, remove from spit to heated platter; remove string. Garnish with corn, parsley, and mushroom-topped tomatoes as pictured. Cut chickens into serving pieces with kitchen scissors. Makes 6 to 8 servings.

HIBACHI CHICKEN

1 3-pound broiler-fryer	¼ cup melted butter or margarine
Paprika	
1 teaspoon salt	2 tablespoons fresh lime juice
¼ teaspoon pepper	
½ teaspoon seasoned salt	3 fresh lime slices

About 1 hour and 30 minutes before serving:

1. Start charcoal fire in hibachi.

2. While waiting for coals to heat up (it takes about 30 minutes), rub inside neck and body cavities and outside surface of chicken with paprika, salt, pepper, and seasoned salt. Now brush chicken with mixture of melted butter and lime juice.

3. Set chicken on hibachi, then grill over hot coals, turning it every few minutes and brushing it often with lime butter, until of desired brownness. Then completely wrap chicken in foil, and grill, turning occasionally, about 60 minutes, or until fork-tender.

4. Remove foil from chicken; brush chicken with remaining lime butter. Garnish with lime slices. Makes 4 servings.

JEWELED CHICKEN
(Pictured opposite)

2 1½- to 2-pound broiler-fryers, halved	½ teaspoon poultry seasoning
Melted butter or margarine	3 eggs, beaten
1 teaspoon seasoned salt	Canned chicken broth
½ teaspoon seasoned pepper	Canned pineapple chunks
1 8-ounce package stuffing mix	Canned pitted dark sweet cherries
1 stalk celery, finely chopped	Seedless green grapes
1 medium onion, minced	Canned mandarin oranges
½ green pepper, finely chopped	Canned diced roasted almonds

About 1 hour and 15 minutes before serving:

1. Start heating oven to 425°F.

2. In shallow, open roasting pan arrange chicken in single layer, skin side up. Brush with melted butter, then sprinkle with seasoned salt and pepper.

3. Bake, uncovered, about 45 minutes, or until fork-tender.

4. Meanwhile, prepare dry stuffing from stuffing mix as label directs; fold in celery, onion, green pepper, poultry seasoning, and eggs. Turn stuffing into buttered 8-by-8-by-2-inch baking dish; cover with foil; bake along

with chicken halves during last 15 minutes of baking time.

5. When chicken is done, with medium ice-cream scoop, place 4 heaping balls of stuffing, lengthwise and equidistantly apart, across large platter. Place second ball of stuffing next to each, forming 4 crosswise rows of stuffing. Now place chicken half over each row of stuffing, alternating legs as pictured. Cover with foil; keep warm in oven, with heat turned off.

6. From drippings in roasting pan make gravy, using canned chicken broth and favorite seasonings.

7. Pour some of hot gravy over each chicken half; top each half with one of fruits; sprinkle all with almonds. Serve hot; pass remaining gravy. Makes 4 servings.

BACON-CHICKEN

2 broiler-fryers, halved	½ cup butter or margarine
1 teaspoon seasoned salt	2 tablespoons Worcester-
¼ teaspoon seasoned	shire
pepper	1 tablespoon lemon juice
8 bacon slices	

About 2 hours before serving:
1. Start heating oven to 350°F.
2. Sprinkle chicken halves with seasoned salt and pepper. With sharp-pointed knife make 3 slits down to bone in each chicken half, one slit starting along thigh to top of drumstick, then two more in breast, equidistantly apart. Tuck long side of 1 bacon slice in slit in thigh; cut second bacon slice in half and tuck into other two slits. Repeat on other halves. Place chicken halves in 15½-by-10½-by-1-inch jelly-roll pan.
3. Melt butter with Worcestershire and lemon juice. Spoon over chicken.
4. Bake about 1 hour and 15 minutes, or until chicken is tender and bacon crisp, basting occasionally with pan juices. Makes 4 servings.

BAKED STUFFED CHICKEN

Melted butter or margarine	1½ cups fresh bread
1 small onion, chopped	crumbs
½ teaspoon salt	½ cup hot water
⅛ teaspoon pepper	1 2½-pound broiler-fryer,
¾ teaspoon poultry	halved
seasoning	2 teaspoons seasoned salt
¼ cup chopped pecans*	

About 1 hour and 15 minutes before serving:
1. Start heating oven to 375°F.
2. In medium skillet, in 1 tablespoon melted butter, sauté onion until lightly browned. Stir in salt, pepper, poultry seasoning, pecans, bread crumbs, and water until smooth.
3. Brush chicken halves with 2 tablespoons melted

butter; sprinkle with seasoned salt. Place chicken halves skin side down, in medium baking dish; top with stuffing.

4. Bake 30 minutes, then turn chicken halves and bake 30 minutes longer, or until golden, basting occasionally. Makes 2 servings.

*You may substitute 1 3- or 4-ounce can sliced mushrooms, drained, or ⅛ pound sausage meat, fried, then broken up.

CHICKEN ITALIANO
(Pictured opposite)

⅓ cup unsifted regular all-purpose flour	½ teaspoon monosodium glutamate
1 teaspoon seasoned salt	Snipped fresh parsley
¼ teaspoon pepper	⅓ cup sherry
2 3-pound broiler-fryers, quartered	1 1-pound package rigoletti macaroni
¼ cup butter or margarine	2 tablespoons salad oil
2 10¼-ounce cans Marinara sauce	8 ounces Mozzarella cheese, sliced

About 2 hours before serving:
1. Combine flour, seasoned salt, and pepper; use to coat chicken pieces well. In melted butter, in skillet, sauté chicken pieces until golden.
2. Start heating oven to 375°F.
3. Place browned chicken in 13-by-9-by-2-inch baking dish. In medium bowl mix Marinara sauce, monosodium glutamate, 2 tablespoons snipped parsley, and sherry; pour over chicken; cover with foil.
4. Bake 45 minutes, then remove foil and bake about 30 minutes longer, or until chicken is almost tender.
5. While chicken bakes, cook rigoletti as package label directs, adding salad oil and stirring occasionally.
6. Arrange cheese slices on chicken as pictured. Continue baking until cheese is melted and bubbly.
7. Place rigoletti in large serving dish; pile chicken on top as pictured. Pour sauce from baking dish around chicken; sprinkle with parsley. Makes 8 servings.

CHICK-N-APPLE
(Pictured on page 53)

4 large red apples	¾ pound small white onions
¾ cup regular all-purpose flour	(8 to 10)
¾ teaspoon ginger	1 2½-pound broiler-fryer, cut up
1½ teaspoons nutmeg	1½ teaspoons salt
Butter or margarine	2 chicken bouillon cubes
	1½ cups water

About 2 hours and 15 minutes before serving:
1. Core, but do not pare apples; cut into rings about ¾ inch thick. Dip in mixture of flour, ginger, and nutmeg. In large skillet, in ¼ cup hot butter, sauté

Chicken Español

Chicken Italiano

apple rings until lightly browned on both sides. Overlap apple rings in diagonal row in 12-by-8-by-2-inch baking dish, making 2 layers.

2. In same skillet sauté whole onions until browned on all sides; set aside.

3. Start heating oven to 350°F.

4. Sprinkle chicken pieces on all sides with salt; dip in flour mixture. Add ¼ cup butter to skillet; in it sauté chicken pieces until well browned. Then arrange chicken pieces and onions on either side of apple rings in baking dish.

5. Stir 2 tablespoons flour mixture into drippings in skillet; add bouillon cubes. Stir in water, a little at a time, blending well. Bring to boil, stirring constantly, then cook 2 or 3 minutes, or until slightly thickened. Pour over apples, chicken, and onions. Cover baking dish with foil.

6. Bake 1 hour and 15 minutes, or until onions and chicken are tender. Serve from baking dish. Makes 4 or 5 servings.

FOR 2: Freezer-wrap half of cut-up chicken; freeze for later use. About 2 hours before serving, prepare rest of chicken and half of other ingredients as directed; bake in 8-by-8-by-2-inch baking dish as above.

CHICKEN FLIP

½ cup regular all-purpose flour	¼ cup snipped celery leaves
1 teaspoon salt	½ pound fresh mushrooms, quartered
½ teaspoon pepper (optional)	2½ cups canned chicken broth
¾ teaspoon poultry seasoning	Dash sage
2 2-pound broiler-fryers, cut up	Dash whole thyme
Butter or margarine	1 teaspoon marjoram
¼ cup chopped onion	2 cups packaged precooked rice
¾ cup chopped celery	

About 2 hours before serving:

1. In brown paper bag or bowl combine flour, salt, ¼ teaspoon pepper, and ½ teaspoon poultry seasoning; use to thoroughly coat chicken pieces (save wings and backs for later use in making soup); in ¼ cup hot butter, in skillet, sauté chicken pieces until golden-brown on all sides. Arrange chicken pieces, skin side down, in lightly greased 13-by-9-by-2-inch baking dish.

2. Start heating oven to 375°F.

3. In same skillet, adding 2 tablespoons butter if needed, sauté onion, celery, celery leaves, and mushrooms 5 minutes. Add 2 cups chicken broth, ¼ teaspoon pepper, sage, thyme, marjoram, ¼ teaspoon poultry seasoning, and rice; bring just to boil. Spread evenly over chicken pieces, packing down firmly. Cover with foil.

4. Bake 30 minutes; then pour on ½ cup chicken broth, re-cover, and bake about 20 minutes longer, or until chicken is fork-tender.

5. Remove foil; let stand 5 minutes, then loosen carefully around edges with spatula; invert on heated serving platter. Or serve right from baking dish. Makes 6 servings.

COQ AU VIN

¼ pound salt pork, diced	½ cup sliced scallions
Boiling water	1 clove garlic, minced
1 3½-pound broiler-fryer, cut up	2 tablespoons regular all-purpose flour
1 teaspoon salt	2 cups red wine
⅛ teaspoon pepper	Snipped parsley
8 small white onions	½ bay leaf
8 small fresh mushrooms	⅛ teaspoon thyme

Day before:

1. In medium Dutch oven cook salt pork in boiling water to cover 5 minutes; drain; then sauté until golden brown. Remove; reserve.

2. In hot fat in Dutch oven sauté chicken pieces until golden on all sides; sprinkle with salt and pepper.

3. Pile chicken on one side of Dutch oven; add onions and mushrooms; simmer, covered, 15 minutes, or until vegetables are golden.

4. Pour off all but about 2 tablespoons fat from Dutch oven; add scallions and garlic; sauté 1 minute. Stir in flour, then slowly stir in wine; cook, stirring constantly, until thickened. Sprinkle with 2 tablespoons parsley, bay leaf, thyme, and salt pork. Cover; refrigerate.

About 1 hour and 10 minutes before serving:

1. Start heating oven to 400°F.

2. Bake chicken, in covered Dutch oven, 1 hour, or until fork-tender.

3. Remove chicken, onions, and mushrooms to heated platter; pour gravy over all; sprinkle with snipped parsley. Makes 6 servings.

CHICKEN IN ORANGE SAUCE

2 2½-pound broiler-fryers, cut up	¼ cup granulated sugar
1½ teaspoons salt	¼ teaspoon dry mustard
Paprika	½ teaspoon cinnamon
¼ cup melted butter or margarine	¼ teaspoon ginger
⅓ cup unsifted regular all-purpose flour	2½ cups orange juice
	1 orange

About 1 hour before serving:

1. Sprinkle chicken pieces with salt and paprika; brown, a few pieces at a time, in melted butter in Dutch oven. Remove.

2. Into drippings in Dutch oven stir flour, sugar,

mustard, cinnamon, and ginger until smooth. Slowly add orange juice; add chicken; simmer, covered, 30 minutes.

3. Meanwhile, with vegetable parer, peel orange. Cut off all membrane. Sliver peel; cover with water; simmer 10 minutes; drain. Section orange.

4. Sprinkle orange peel over chicken; add orange sections; cook, covered, 10 minutes, or until chicken is fork-tender. Serve chicken pieces with sauce. Makes 8 servings.

CHICKEN AND SCAMPI
(Pictured on page 46)

1 3½- to 4-pound broiler-fryer, cut up	3 tablespoons snipped parsley
1 tablespoon salt	½ cup port wine
½ teaspoon pepper	1 8-ounce can tomato sauce
¼ cup butter or margarine	1 teaspoon basil
3 small onions, finely chopped	1 pound shelled, deveined shrimp
1 clove garlic, minced	Snipped parsley

About 45 minutes before serving:

1. Rub chicken pieces well with salt and pepper. In hot butter, in large skillet, sauté chicken until golden on all sides.
2. Now add onions, garlic, 3 tablespoons parsley, wine, tomato sauce, and basil; simmer, covered, about 30 minutes, or until chicken is tender.
3. Push chicken pieces to one side of skillet; turn up heat so tomato mixture boils; add shrimp, then cook, uncovered, 3 or 4 minutes, or until just pink and tender.
4. Pile chicken pieces in serving dish; top with shrimp. If necessary skim all fat from sauce; pour sauce over chicken and shrimp. Sprinkle with snipped parsley. Makes 6 servings.

HOT-AND-SPICY CHICKEN

½ cup butter or margarine	2 8-ounce cans tomato sauce
1 3- to 4-pound broiler-fryer, cut up	1 to 2 teaspoons chili powder
1 green pepper, chopped	2 teaspoons salt
1 onion, chopped	¼ teaspoon Tabasco
1 clove garlic, minced	2 whole cloves

About 1 hour and 10 minutes before serving:

1. In hot butter, in Dutch oven or large skillet, sauté chicken pieces until well browned; remove.
2. To drippings in Dutch oven add green pepper, onion, and garlic; cook until lightly browned; drain off excess fat.
3. Combine tomato sauce, chili powder, salt, Tabasco, and cloves. Return chicken to Dutch oven; spoon some tomato mixture over each piece. Simmer, covered, about 45 minutes, or until chicken is fork-tender.

4. Serve with hot, fluffy mashed potatoes or rice, passing extra sauce. Nice with sautéed pineapple slices, buttered spinach, and apple tapioca. Makes 4 or 5 servings.

CREAMED CHICKEN À LA REINE

2 chicken breasts, split in half	1 tablespoon regular all-purpose flour
½ teaspoon seasoned salt	2½ cups water
2 tablespoons butter or margarine	½ teaspoon curry powder
1 medium onion, sliced	½ teaspoon basil
1 package Swiss chicken-noodle-soup mix*	⅓ cup commercial sour cream

About 1 hour and 15 minutes before serving:

1. Start heating oven to 350°F.
2. Sprinkle chicken breasts with seasoned salt. In hot butter, in large skillet, brown chicken breasts and onion well. Transfer to 1½-quart baking dish.
3. To drippings add soup mix, flour, water, curry powder, and basil; stir, bring to boil. With wire whip beat in sour cream until smooth. Pour over chicken breasts.
4. Bake, covered, 1 hour, or until tender. Serve with mashed potatoes. Makes 4 servings.
*You may substitute 1 1⅝-ounce can dehydrated cream-of-mushroom soup for chicken-noodle-soup mix, using only ½ tablespoon flour.

CHICKEN PARMIGIANA
(Pictured on page 46)

1 4-serving portion dry instant potato flakes	¼ pound spaghetti
1 teaspoon salt	4 processed Swiss-cheese slices
¼ teaspoon pepper	1 1-pound can stewed tomatoes
1 egg	¼ cup grated Parmesan cheese
2 tablespoons water	Parsley sprigs
2 chicken breasts, split in half	
Butter or margarine	

About 1 hour and 20 minutes before serving:

1. Start heating oven to 350°F.

Chicken Parmigiana

Chicken and Scampi

Mix dry potato flakes with salt and pepper. Beat egg with water; in it dip chicken breasts; then coat well with potato-flake mixture.

In oven, in large shallow baking dish, heat ¼ cup butter until hot. In it lay chicken breasts, skin side down. Bake 25 minutes; turn over and bake about 20 minutes longer, or until golden.

Meanwhile, cook spaghetti as package label directs

Turn oven heat to 500°F. Remove chicken from oven; place folded slice Swiss cheese on each piece. Then return to oven for 10 minutes, or until cheese is melted.

Meanwhile, heat stewed tomatoes. Toss spaghetti with Parmesan cheese and 3 tablespoons butter. Arrange on serving dish. Top with chicken; spoon tomatoes round; garnish with parsley sprigs. Makes 3 servings.

CHICKEN ESPAÑOL
(Pictured on page 43)

⅓ cup unsifted regular
  all-purpose flour
Seasoned salt
¼ teaspoon pepper
  teaspoon paprika
6 chicken drumsticks
6 chicken thighs
6 chicken wings
Butter or margarine
1 large green pepper,
  slivered
1 1-pound 10-ounce can
  whole tomatoes, drained,
  chopped

1 teaspoon monosodium
  glutamate
1 1-pound package large
  macaroni shells
¼ teaspoon saffron
1 9-ounce package frozen
  artichoke hearts
1 dozen cherrystone clams,
  in shells
½ pound fresh shrimp,
  shelled, deveined

About 2 hours and 30 minutes before serving:

1. Combine flour with 2 teaspoons seasoned salt, pepper, and paprika; use to coat all chicken pieces on all sides.

2. In ¼ cup melted buter, in 8-quart Dutch oven, sauté chicken until golden on all sides; add green pepper, tomatoes, and monosodium glutamate. Cook, covered, over medium heat, 45 minutes, stirring tomato mixture occasionally.

3. Start heating oven to 375°F.

4. Boil macaroni shells as package label directs about 10 minutes, or until partially tender; drain. Mix saffron with 2 tablespoons hot water; stir into macaroni. Now toss macaroni with chicken in Dutch oven.

5. Bake, uncovered, 30 minutes.

6. Meanwhile, cook artichoke hearts as package label directs; also steam clams, in a little water, until their shells open—about 10 minutes.

7. In 2 tablespoons melted butter, sauté shrimp, sprinkled with ½ teaspoon seasoned salt, until they are pink and tender—about 3 to 5 minutes.

8. To serve, arrange chicken pieces and macaroni shells on large platter; garnish with artichoke hearts, clams, and shrimp as pictured. Makes 8 servings.

CHICKEN À LA BENEDICT
(Pictured on page 49)

¼ cup unsifted regular
  all-purpose flour
¼ teaspoon pepper
1 teaspoon paprika
5 chicken breasts, boned,
  skinned, halved
Butter or margarine

10 slices Canadian-style
  bacon, ¼ inch thick
5 English muffins, split
About 1 cup Hollandaise
  sauce, bottled or
  homemade

About 1 hour and 30 minutes before serving:

1. Start heating oven to 325°F.

2. Mix flour with pepper and paprika; use to coat chicken breasts. Then, in ¼ cup hot butter, in large skillet, sauté breasts until golden.

3. Place chicken breasts in 13-by-9-by-2-inch baking dish; add drippings from skillet. Cover with foil.

4. Bake 25 minutes; remove foil, turn chicken breasts; bake about 10 minutes longer, or until tender; keep warm.

5. Preheat broiler 10 minutes, or as manufacturer directs.

6. Meanwhile, sauté bacon slices in 1 tablespoon butter until golden; keep warm. Butter split muffins; arrange on cookie sheet. Broil, 4 inches from heat, until nicely toasted.

7. Then, on each muffin half, place a bacon slice, then a chicken piece, with same side up as in baking dish. Top with heaping teaspoon Hollandaise. Broil, 6 inches from heat, about 3 minutes, or until sauce is bubbly. Makes 10 servings.

DRUMSTICK CROWN
(Pictured on page 40)

¼ cup unsifted regular
  all-purpose flour
¾ teaspoon salt
⅛ teaspoon pepper
1 teaspoon paprika
8 chicken drumsticks
¼ cup butter or margarine

1 8½-ounce can pine-
  apple slices
1½ cups uncooked regular
  white rice
1 ripe avocado
2 tablespoons lemon juice
½ pound blue grapes

About 50 minutes before serving:

1. On paper plate combine flour, salt, pepper, and paprika; use to coat drumsticks on all sides. In large skillet, in hot butter, sauté drumsticks until golden brown on all sides. Now add syrup from pineapple slices. Simmer, covered, about 30 to 40 minutes, or until chicken is tender.

2. Meanwhile, cook rice as package label directs; keep hot.

3. Peel avocado; cut in half crosswise; remove pit; then slice into 4 slices, ¾ inch thick; cut slices in half. Brush with lemon juice. Rinse grapes, then separate them. Cut 4 pineapple slices in half.

4. When drumsticks are tender, mound rice in center of heated serving plate. Place drumsticks in circle, equidistantly apart, up against rice. Arrange a pineapple and avocado slice under every drumstick. Garnish with a few grapes as pictured. Makes 4 servings.

POT-ROASTED CHICKEN THIGHS

Butter or margarine	½ cup unsifted regular
½ pound fresh mushrooms, halved	all-purpose flour
	Salt
12 tiny white onions	1 teaspoon paprika
12 tiny new potatoes, scrubbed, dried	½ teaspoon pepper
	12 chicken thighs
	Snipped fresh parsley

About 1 hour and 15 minutes before serving:

1. In ⅓ cup hot butter, in Dutch oven, sauté mushrooms until golden, removing when done. In same butter sauté onions until browned, then remove.

2. In ¼ cup butter, in medium skillet, sauté potatoes until browned.

3. Meanwhile, combine flour, 1 teaspoon salt, paprika, and pepper; use to coat chicken. Reheat butter in Dutch oven; in it sauté chicken thighs until golden on all sides, adding more butter if needed; sprinkle with 1 teaspoon salt.

4. Add sautéed mushrooms, onions, and potatoes to chicken in Dutch oven; cook, covered, over low heat, 20 to 25 minutes, or until chicken is done and potatoes are tender, stirring once or twice. Sprinkle with snipped parsley; serve hot. Makes 4 to 6 servings.

GLAZED CHICKEN WINGS
(Pictured on page 40)

6 pairs of chicken wings (about 3 pounds)	1 12-ounce jar apricot preserves
Salt	⅓ cup prepared mustard
Pepper	¼ cup brown sugar, packed
Flour	Wild rice
½ cup butter or margarine	White rice
1 10½-ounce can condensed beef broth, undiluted	Canned cling-peach slices (optional)
	Whole peeled apricots (optional)

About 1 hour and 30 minutes before serving:

1. Over gas flame or with match, singe chicken wings free of all hairs. Sprinkle wings with salt, pepper, and flour.

2. In hot butter, in Dutch oven, sauté chicken wings until very well browned on all sides, turning as needed.

Add broth; cover and cook until largest wing is fork-tender.

3. Meanwhile, in small saucepan make glaze: Over low heat stir together apricot preserves, mustard, brown sugar, ½ teaspoon salt, ¼ teaspoon pepper until bubbly. Line large cookie sheet with foil. Start cooking rice as package label directs.*

4. Preheat broiler 10 minutes, or as manufacturer directs.

5. Place chicken wings on foil-lined cookie sheet; brush liberally with glaze.

6. Broil until bubbly and well browned; turn wings, brush again with glaze, then broil as before.

7. Pile rice in center of heated platter; place chicken wings around it, with peach slices around wings; then pile whole apricots on top. Pass remaining glaze. Makes 4 to 6 servings.

*We used 1 cup each of uncooked wild rice and processed white rice.

GOLDEN CHICKEN WINGS

2 pounds chicken wings	1 10½-ounce can condensed cream-of-chicken soup, undiluted
¼ cup unsifted regular all-purpose flour	
1 teaspoon salt	1 cup water
1 teaspoon paprika	1 1-pound can cling-peach slices, drained
¼ cup butter or margarine	
2 teaspoons curry powder	Slivered toasted almonds

About 50 minutes before serving:

1. Over gas flame or match, singe chicken wings free of all hairs. Combine flour, salt, and paprika; use to coat chicken wings evenly.

2. In hot butter, in large skillet, sauté wings until golden on all sides. Sprinkle with curry powder; stir in soup and water; simmer, covered, 40 minutes, or until wings are fork-tender.

3. Add peach slices; heat 5 minutes. Sprinkle with almonds. Makes 4 servings.

CHICKEN SANTA FE
(Pictured opposite)

¼ cup salad oil	2 1-pound 1-ounce cans kidney beans, drained
1 4- to 5-pound ready-to-cook roaster, cut up	
	1 12-ounce can whole-kernel corn
2 onions, sliced	
2 cups water	1 1-pound can Blue Lake cut green beans
5 teaspoons salt	
½ to 1 teaspoon pepper	1 16- to 17-ounce can tomatoes
½ teaspoon whole sage	
8 ounces elbow macaroni	4 dashes Tabasco

About 2 hours and 30 minutes before serving:

1. In hot salad oil, in 7-quart Dutch oven or kettle, brown chicken pieces well. Add onions and sauté until

Chicken Santa Fe

Chicken Ring

Chicken-in-Omelet Pinwheel

Chicken à la Benedict

golden. Then add water, salt, pepper, and sage. Cook, covered, about 2 hours, or until chicken is fork-tender.

2. Meanwhile, cook elbow macaroni as package label directs; drain.

3. When chicken is tender, add kidney beans, corn, green beans, tomatoes, macaroni, and Tabasco; heat. Serve in rimmed soup plates, if desired. Nice with warmed French bread, tossed endive salad, and, for dessert, Concord grapes. Makes 8 servings.

SUMPTUOUS CHICKEN STEW
(Pictured on page 11)

2 2½- to 3-pound broiler-
  fryers, cut up
½ cup regular all-purpose
  flour
2 teaspoons paprika
Salt
¼ teaspoon pepper
Butter or margarine
4 large onions, sliced
4 cups canned chicken
  broth
1 teaspoon whole tarragon
1 teaspoon whole basil

1 large bunch carrots
  (about 10)
6 stalks celery
1 pound fresh mushrooms
2 tablespoons lemon juice
½ pound fully-cooked ham,
  in one piece
8 slices fresh white
  bread
1 cup light cream
2 egg yolks
⅔ to 1 cup sherry
1 pound new potatoes
  (optional)

About 2 hours before serving:

1. Coat chicken pieces well with combined flour, paprika, 1½ teaspoons salt, and pepper. (Reserve remaining flour mixture.) In 3 tablespoons hot butter, in large Dutch oven, over medium heat, sauté chicken pieces until crisp golden-brown.

2. Add onions and cook until lightly browned. Stir in chicken broth, tarragon, basil, and 1 teaspoon salt. Simmer, covered, 15 minutes.

3. Meanwhile, cut each carrot diagonally into 3 or 4 pieces. Slice celery diagonally about ¼ inch thick. Quarter or slice mushrooms; sprinkle with lemon juice; cover, then refrigerate until needed.

4. Add carrots to stew; simmer 20 minutes.

5. Meanwhile, cut ham into about 30 cubes, each 1 inch by ½ inch; then sauté in 1 tablespoon butter until browned. Add ham, celery, mushrooms, and lemon juice to stew. Cook about 15 to 20 minutes, or until all are fork-tender.

6. Meanwhile, from bread slices, with 2-inch round cookie cutter, cut about 16 2-inch circles. In about ¼ cup butter, in skillet, sauté bread rounds until crisp on both sides; keep warm.

7. Combine cream, egg yolks, and reserved flour mixture. Arrange chicken and vegetables in large casserole; keep warm.

8. Into gravy, in Dutch oven, stir cream mixture and sherry; bring *just* to boil; pour some over chicken. Gar-nish with bread rounds; serve. Pass rest of gravy and boiled new potatoes, if desired. Makes about 8 servings.

FOR 4: Halve all ingredients above and proceed as directed.

CHICKEN-IN-OMELET PINWHEEL
(Pictured on page 49)

1 2½- to 3-pound broiler-
  fryer
3 cups hot water
Salt
Salad oil
Butter or margarine
Sifted regular all-purpose
  flour
Dash cayenne pepper
1½ cups milk
4 eggs, separated
6 small fresh mushrooms
2 stalks celery, diced
½ cup slivered blanched
  almonds

2 tablespoons chopped
  canned pimentos
1 tablespoon lemon juice
½ teaspoon seasoned salt
½ teaspoon monosodium
  glutamate
½ teaspoon onion salt
⅓ cup commercial sour
  cream
6 large ripe olives
1 9-ounce package frozen
  French-style green
  beans

Day before:

Simmer chicken in hot water with 1 tablespoon salt about 1½ hours, or until fork-tender. Remove chicken; strain broth; refrigerate. Remove chicken meat in small pieces from bones; refrigerate it, covered, until needed next day.

About 1 hour and 15 minutes before serving:

1. Grease 15½-by-10½-by-1-inch jelly-roll pan with salad oil; line with wax paper; butter wax paper; dust with flour.

2. Sift together ½ cup sifted regular all-purpose flour, ½ teaspoon salt, and cayenne.

3. In medium saucepan, over low heat, melt ¼ cup butter; remove from heat. With wire whisk or 4-tined fork blend in flour mixture; then stir in milk gradually. Cook over medium-high heat, stirring constantly, until it boils 1 minute. Remove from heat.

4. Start heating oven to 325°F.

5. In small bowl, with mixer at high speed, beat egg whites *just* until stiff, but still moist. Beat egg yolks slightly; stir some of hot sauce into yolks, then stir yolk mixture into hot sauce. Fold this hot mixture gradually into egg whites until no streaks remain; spread evenly in jelly-roll pan.

6. Bake 45 to 50 minutes, or until top is golden brown and springs back when lightly pressed with finger.

7. Meanwhile, remove stems from mushrooms; slice stems into large bowl; mix in chicken, celery, almonds, pimentos, lemon juice, seasoned salt, monosodium gluta-mate, onion salt, and sour cream. In medium saucepan, over low heat, heat this salad mixture, but do not let it boil.

8. If desired, flute mushroom caps with sharp knife by removing 4 or 5 thin strips, equidistantly, from around top of each. In 2 tablespoons melted butter, in medium skillet, sauté caps until golden; skewer each with a ripe olive on toothpick as pictured. Then make favorite gravy using 1 cup reserved broth; also cook beans as package label directs.

9. When omelet is done, loosen edges with spatula; cover with wax paper; place large cookie sheet on top, then quickly invert; lift off pan; peel off wax paper. Spoon salad mixture evenly over omelet. Starting at crosswise end, roll up omelet, jelly-roll fashion, lifting wax paper as you roll to guide it.

10. With 2 wide spatulas lift omelet roll to heated platter; garnish with ripe olives and fluted mushroom caps as pictured. Surround with green beans. Serve, sliced; pass gravy in a pitcher or gravy boat. Makes 6 servings.

CHICKEN RING
(Pictured on page 49)

2 tablespoons butter or margarine	1 cup cooked or canned peas, drained
½ cup chopped onion	1 teaspoon salt
2 cups cooked chicken, in small pieces	4 cups packaged biscuit mix
½ cup chopped ripe olives	1⅓ cups milk
¼ cup diced pimento	1 egg, beaten
	Herbed Gravy, below

About 1 hour before serving:

1. In hot butter, in skillet, sauté onion until tender; add chicken, olives, pimento, peas, and salt; heat.
2. Start heating oven to 425°F.
3. In bowl combine biscuit mix with milk. Turn out onto lightly-floured surface; knead 8 to 10 times. Then roll into rectangle 20 by 10 inches; spoon chicken mixture evenly down center of dough; fold lengthwise over mixture until edges meet; pinch edges together. Place, seam side down, on greased cookie sheet. Shape into a ring; pinch ends together; with kitchen scissors, cut through ring at 1-inch intervals, from outer edge almost to center, making 1-inch slices. Turn each slice slightly so filling shows. Brush with beaten egg.
4. Bake 25 to 30 minutes, or until golden.
5. Meanwhile, make Herbed Gravy; keep warm. Loosen ring from cookie sheet; slide onto heated platter; serve, passing gravy. Makes 8 servings.

HERBED GRAVY: In 2 tablespoons melted butter or margarine, in saucepan, sauté 2 tablespoons minced onion until tender; add ½ teaspoon tarragon and 2 teaspoons basil. Stir in 2 packages golden- or light-gravy mix. Then, stirring constantly, add 1½ cups water and 2 cups milk. Bring to boil; simmer, stirring, until thickened.

CAPE HORN COD

2 cod steaks (about 1 pound), or 1 1-pound package frozen cod fillets, thawed	3 tablespoons butter or margarine
2 eggs, beaten	½ envelope tomato-soup mix
Packaged flavored bread crumbs	1 tablespoon Worcestershire
	1½ teaspoons lemon juice
	1 tablespoon onion-soup mix

About 45 minutes before serving:

1. Dip cod steaks in beaten eggs, then in bread crumbs, until well coated on all sides.
2. In large skillet, over medium-high heat, melt butter; in it sauté fish until golden-brown on both sides, and easily flaked with fork, *but still moist*, turning once. Then arrange fish on platter; keep warm.
3. Meanwhile, in saucepan, combine tomato-soup mix, 1 cup water, Worcestershire, lemon juice, and onion-soup mix. Heat to boiling; pour at once over fish and serve. Makes 2 or 3 servings.

LEMON-FISH SAUTÉ

1 egg	¼ pound butter or margarine
¾ cup wheat germ (in jar)	Lemon wedges
⅛ teaspoon pepper	
1 pound frozen fillets of flounder or sole, thawed	

About 30 minutes before serving:

1. In small bowl, with fork, beat egg with 2 tablespoons water until blended. In pie plate combine wheat germ with pepper. Pat thawed fillets dry with paper towels.
2. Dip fillets, one at a time, in egg, then coat with wheat germ.
3. In large skillet, heat butter; in it quickly sauté

fillets, turning once, until golden and easily flaked with fork, *but still moist*. Serve with lemon wedges. Makes 3 servings.

SPANISH COD STEAKS

Butter or margarine	Salt
1 large onion, sliced	2 cod steaks, ¾ inch thick
1 1-pound can tomatoes	Pepper
⅛ teaspoon whole orégano	1 tablespoon lemon juice

About 45 minutes before serving:

1. In 1 tablespoon hot butter sauté onion; stir in tomatoes, orégano, and ½ teaspoon salt. Simmer, uncovered, 30 minutes.
2. Meanwhile, start heating oven to 350°F.
3. Remove bone from cod steaks; lay steaks in 10-by-6-by-2-inch baking dish; sprinkle with pepper, ½ teaspoon salt, and lemon juice; dot with 1 tablespoon butter.
4. Bake 25 minutes; then pour on onion-tomato mixture and bake 5 minutes longer, or until fish flakes easily, *but is still moist*. Makes 2 servings.

CORAL BAKE

1 pound fresh or thawed frozen flounder fillets	2 tablespoons chopped onion
Salt	1 bay leaf
Pepper	Pinch sage
¼ cup melted butter or margarine	1 8-ounce can tomato sauce
	¼ cup water

1. Start heating oven to 350°F.
2. Place flounder fillets, side by side, in greased shallow baking dish. Lightly season with salt and pepper.
3. Combine melted butter with onion, 1 teaspoon salt, ¼ teaspoon pepper, bay leaf, sage, tomato sauce, and water; pour over fish.
4. Bake 35 to 40 minutes, or until fish flakes easily with fork, *but is still moist*. Makes 4 servings.

GOURMET FLOUNDER

1¼ pounds flounder fillets (4 pieces)	2 tablespoons lemon juice
Salt	½ teaspoon granulated sugar
¼ teaspoon seasoned pepper	⅛ teaspoon white pepper
Fresh dill	2 tablespoons snipped chives
⅓ cup milk	½ cup finely-chopped cucumber
½ cup commercial sour cream	

Early on day:

1. Start heating oven to 350°F.
2. Sprinkle flounder fillets with 1 teaspoon salt, seasoned pepper, and 1 tablespoon snipped dill. Lay, side by side, in 12-by-8-by-2-inch baking dish; pour milk over fish.
3. Bake 25 minutes.
4. Let flounder cool in milk; then, with wide spatula, remove drained fillets to serving platter. Refrigerate, covered, at least 3 hours.
5. Meanwhile, in small bowl combine sour cream, lemon juice, sugar, ½ teaspoon salt, white pepper, 1 tablespoon snipped dill, chives, and cucumber. Refrigerate.

About 5 minutes before serving:

In center of each flounder fillet, place heaping tablespoonful of sour-cream sauce; pass rest. Garnish platter with dill sprigs. Makes 4 servings.

HADDOCK BAKE

1 teaspoon salt	½ cup milk
¼ teaspoon pepper	½ cup commercial sour cream
¼ cup unsifted regular all-purpose flour	½ cup finely-crushed packaged cheese crackers
1 pound frozen haddock fillets, thawed	Parsley sprigs

About 1 hour before serving:

1. Start heating oven to 350°F.
2. On wax paper combine salt, pepper, and flour. Use to coat fish fillets on all sides. Lay fillets in greased 10-by-6-by-2-inch baking dish; pour on milk.
3. Bake, uncovered, 30 to 35 minutes, or until fish flakes easily, *but is still moist*.
4. Then spoon sour cream over fillets; sprinkle with cheese-cracker crumbs. Bake 10 minutes longer. Serve garnished with parsley sprigs. Makes 4 servings.

BAKED FLOUNDER FILLETS SUPREME
(Pictured opposite)

6 large flounder fillets (about 2 pounds)	2 small onions, sliced
Seasoned salt	1½ tablespoons regular all-purpose flour
1 medium tomato	Snipped parsley
6 slices natural Swiss cheese	1 cup light cream
1 3- or 4-ounce can sliced mushrooms	6 tablespoons sherry
2 tablespoons butter or margarine	2 cups packaged precooked rice

About 45 minutes before serving:

1. Sprinkle flounder fillets lightly on both sides with seasoned salt, then roll up each. Cut tomato into 6 slices; fold cheese slices in half crosswise. Now arrange flounder rolls, tomato slices, and cheese slices alternately down center of 13-by-9-by-2-inch baking dish.
2. Start heating oven to 400°F.
3. Drain mushrooms, reserving liquid. In large skillet,

Lemon-Butter-Broiled Salmon Steak

Chick-n-Apple, Flounder Fillets Supreme

in hot butter sauté mushrooms and onions until golden. Stir in flour, 1½ teaspoons seasoned salt, and ¼ cup snipped parsley; then add cream, mushroom liquid combined with enough water to measure ½ cup, and sherry, stirring until mixed. Bring to boil; pour over fish.

4. Bake 20 minutes, or until fillets are golden and easily flaked with fork, *but still moist.*

5. Meanwhile, prepare rice as package label directs; then stir in ½ cup snipped parsley. When fish is done, spoon rice along its sides. Makes 6 servings.

SURPRISE PARCELS

3 pounds frozen fish
   fillets (cod, flounder,
   or sole), thawed
Butter or margarine
Seasoned salt
Seasoned pepper
Instant minced onion

Snipped fresh dill
12 tomato wedges
2 hard-cooked eggs,
   sliced
12 raw shrimp, shelled,
   deveined

About 45 minutes before serving:

1. Start heating oven to 450°F.

2. Pat fish fillets dry with paper towels; arrange on 6 14-inch squares of foil, dividing fillets evenly among the six packages.

3. On fillets in each package, place ½ tablespoon butter, then sprinkle with ¼ teaspoon seasoned salt, a little seasoned pepper, ¼ teaspoon instant minced onion, and 1 tablespoon snipped dill.

4. Also, on fillets, arrange tomato wedges, egg slices, and shrimp, dividing equally. Wrap foil loosely around fillets; lay, seam-side up, on jelly-roll pan.

5. Bake 20 to 25 minutes, or until fish flakes easily with fork, *but is still moist.*

6. Serve one parcel, unopened, to each person. Pass mashed potatoes and broccoli. Makes 6 servings.

LEMON-BUTTER-BROILED
SALMON STEAKS
(Pictured on page 53)

¼ cup mayonnaise or
   cooked salad dressing
2 teaspoons prepared
   mustard
2 tablespoons butter or
   margarine
1 tablespoon lemon juice
1 teaspoon paprika

⅛ teaspoon marjoram
⅛ teaspoon pepper
2 fresh salmon steaks, ¾
   inch thick
2 tablespoons snipped
   parsley
2 lemon twists

About 35 minutes before serving:

1. Preheat broiler 10 minutes, or as manufacturer directs.

2. Into mayonnaise stir mustard; set aside. In small saucepan, over low heat, melt butter; blend in lemon juice, paprika, marjoram, and pepper.

3. Lay salmon steaks on foil-lined broiler pan; brush with butter mixture.

4. Broil, about 2 inches from heat, 8 minutes, or until golden, brushing once with butter mixture. Turn; brush with butter mixture, then broil 5 to 7 minutes, or until fish flakes easily, *but is still moist.*

5. Serve, sprinkled with parsley and garnished with lemon twists; pass mustard-mayonnaise. Makes 2 servings.

SALMON LOAF, WEST-COAST STYLE

1 1-pound can salmon,
   drained (2 cups)
¾ cup fresh bread crumbs
1 egg, slightly beaten
¾ cup milk
2 tablespoons minced onion
Salt

⅛ teaspoon pepper
2 tablespoons melted butter
   or margarine
3 tablespoons lemon juice
¼ cup melted butter or
   margarine
¼ cup lemon juice

1. Start heating oven to 350°F.

2. Combine salmon, bread crumbs, egg, milk, onion, ½ teaspoon salt, pepper, 2 tablespoons melted butter, and 3 tablespoons lemon juice; toss with fork. Turn into greased 9-by-5-by-3-inch loaf pan.

3. Bake 40 to 55 minutes, or until done.

4. Meanwhile, for sauce, combine ¼ cup melted butter, ¼ cup lemon juice, and ⅛ teaspoon salt.

5. To serve, pour sauce over salmon loaf in pan. Or serve loaf and sauce separately. Makes 4 servings.

TUNA CORN-BREAD PIE

12 thin lemon slices
1 6½- or 7-ounce can
   tuna
½ cup fresh bread crumbs
2 tablespoons minced onion
2 eggs, beaten

1 10½-ounce can con-
   densed cream-of-mush-
   room soup, undiluted
1 package corn-muffin or
   corn-bread mix
Snipped parsley

About 45 minutes before serving:

1. Arrange lemon slices in bottom of lightly-greased 10-inch pie plate.

2. Drain, then flake, tuna; blend well with bread crumbs, onion, eggs, and soup. Spoon into pie plate over lemon slices.

3. Start heating oven to 400°F.

4. Prepare corn-muffin mix as package label directs; spoon gently over tuna mixture until level with inner edge of pie-plate rim (turn any excess into custard cup).

5. Bake 30 minutes, or until golden.

6. Let cool 10 minutes. Then, with spatula, loosen sides of pie. Invert serving dish on top of pie, then invert both, unmolding pie, bottom side up. Sprinkle with snipped parsley. Makes 4 or 5 servings.

TUNA-VEGETABLE BAKE

½ 10½-ounce can con-
densed cream-of-mush-
room or cream-of-celery
soup, undiluted
2 tablespoons milk
1 6½- or 7-ounce can
tuna, drained
½ cup grated Cheddar
cheese

⅛ teaspoon whole orégano
⅛ teaspoon dry mustard
Dash Tabasco
Speck pepper
1 8¼-ounce can mixed
vegetables, drained
Toasted split English
muffins or hot fluffy
rice

About 20 minutes before serving:

1. In electric skillet at 200°F., or in large skillet, over low heat, combine all ingredients except English muffins; heat.

2. Serve over English muffins or hot fluffy rice. Makes 2 servings.

TUNA-SESAME ROLL CASSEROLE

1 10-ounce package frozen
peas
¼ cup butter or margarine
1 9¼-ounce package
refrigerated sesame
dinner rolls
1 tablespoon shredded
Parmesan cheese
1 3- or 4-ounce can sliced
mushrooms

1 medium onion, sliced, or
2 tablespoons minced
onion
2 6½- or 7-ounce cans
tuna
1 10½-ounce can con-
densed cream-of-mush-
room soup, undiluted
1 canned pimento, cut up
(optional)

About 30 minutes before serving:

1. Cook peas in ⅓ cup boiling water, covered, omitting salt, 3 minutes. In small skillet melt butter.

2. Start heating oven to 400°F.

3. Open package of rolls as directed; cut dough along marks into 12 pieces. Dip top of each in melted butter; then arrange, slightly overlapping, down long sides of 12-by-8-by-2-inch baking dish. Sprinkle with cheese.

4. Bake 15 minutes, or until golden.

5. Meanwhile, drain mushrooms, reserving liquid; brown onion and mushrooms in remaining butter.

6. In small saucepan combine tuna with soup, mush-

room liquid, onion-mushroom mixture, and pimento; heat; add peas. Turn into center of casserole; serve. Makes 6 servings.

TUNA-STUFFED-CABBAGE ROLLS

1 large head green cabbage
2 6½- or 7-ounce cans tuna
1 cup cooked rice
1 cup minced celery
½ cup minced onion
1 tablespoon prepared
mustard
2 teaspoons caraway seeds
1 egg
2 cups canned chicken broth

1 tablespoon brown sugar
½ cup light cream
2 tablespoons regular all-
purpose flour
¼ teaspoon salt
¼ teaspoon nutmeg
⅛ teaspoon pepper
3 tablespoons prepared
horse-radish

About 45 minutes before serving:

1. Carefully remove 12 large leaves from cabbage. Cook leaves in boiling salted water 2 minutes; drain; cool. Make 2-inch lengthwise cut through heavy vein of each leaf.

2. In large bowl coarsely flake tuna; add rice, celery, onion, mustard, and caraway seeds. With fork slightly beat egg; blend into tuna mixture.

3. On each cabbage leaf place ⅓ cup tuna mixture; fold sides of cabbage over tuna, tucking them in securely; fasten with toothpick.

4. Place rolls in large skillet; pour on chicken broth, then sprinkle with brown sugar. Bring to boil; simmer, covered, 15 to 20 minutes, or until cabbage rolls are tender. Remove rolls to deep serving dish.

5. Mix cream and flour to smooth paste; gradually stir into hot liquid in skillet. Then stir in salt, nutmeg, pepper, and horse-radish; cook, stirring constantly, until thickened. Pour over cabbage rolls. Makes 6 servings.

SOUTHERN CRAB CAKES

3 cups cooked fresh, or
thawed frozen or canned
King-crab meat, drained
1½ teaspoons salt
1 teaspoon dry mustard
½ teaspoon pepper
1 egg yolk
2 teaspoons Worcestershire

1 tablespoon mayonnaise
2 teaspoons snipped parsley
Flour
1 egg, slightly beaten
2 tablespoons water
Packaged dried bread
crumbs
Butter or margarine

1. Mix together crab meat, salt, mustard, pepper, egg yolk, Worcestershire, mayonnaise, and parsley. Press firmly into 8 small cakes. Refrigerate until well chilled.

2. Just before serving, dip cakes in flour; then into egg combined with water; then into crumbs.

3. In skillet melt a little butter; in it, over high heat, sauté cakes rapidly until delicate brown.

4. Serve with potato salad, coleslaw, or French fries. Or serve on hot toasted rolls. Makes 4 servings.

CRAB MEAT À LA NOME

2⅔ cups cooked fresh or
   thawed frozen or canned
   King-crab meat, drained
1 egg yolk, beaten
½ cup heavy cream
½ teaspoon salt

⅛ teaspoon pepper
6 slices bread
4 tablespoons melted
   butter or margarine
½ cup fresh bread crumbs
Parsley

1. Start heating oven to 400°F.
2. Combine crab meat with egg yolk, cream, salt, and pepper. Brush bread slices on one side with 3 tablespoons melted butter; then sauté on buttered side in skillet until golden. Or arrange, after buttering, in greased baking dish, unbuttered side up.
3. Heap crab-meat mixture on top of bread; sprinkle with bread crumbs combined with 1 tablespoon melted butter.
4. Bake 10 minutes; then garnish with parsley and serve. Makes 6 servings.

CURRIED-LOBSTER SCRAMBLE

6 eggs
¼ cup light cream
½ teaspoon onion salt
2 tablespoons butter or
   margarine
½ teaspoon curry powder

2 cups well-drained cooked
   lobster meat
4 slices white bread
Catchup
Water cress or parsley

About 20 minutes before serving:

1. Lightly beat eggs with cream and onion salt. In skillet, over low heat, melt butter; stir in curry powder and lobster meat; heat. Toast bread, cut in halves.
2. Meanwhile, pour egg mixture into skillet; then toss with lobster while eggs cook to desired degree of doneness.
3. Spread catchup on toast halves, then heap curried-lobster mixture on them. Garnish with water cress. Makes 4 servings.

ROCK-LOBSTER RICE

8 5-ounce or 4 9-ounce frozen rock-lobster tails
2 cups cooked packaged
   precooked rice
¼ cup butter or margarine
2 tablespoons regular all-
   purpose flour
1 cup light cream

¾ teaspoon salt
Dash pepper
2 dashes Angostura bitters
¼ cup sherry
Paprika
Lime wedges
Preserved guava shells
   (optional)

1. Boil lobster tails as package label directs. Remove meat from shells; cut into 1½-inch chunks; set lobster meat and shells aside.
2. Preheat broiler 10 minutes, or as manufacturer directs.
3. Line lobster shells with a thin layer of rice. Put rest of rice in large bowl; add lobster meat, reserving some especially choice pieces for topping.
4. In small saucepan, over medium heat, melt butter; stir in flour, cream, salt, pepper, and bitters. Cook, stirring, until thickened; then stir in sherry. Pour sauce over rice and lobster; toss lightly. Pile in rice-lined shells; top with reserved lobster pieces.
5. Broil, about 4 inches from heat, 4 minutes, or until nicely browned.
6. Sprinkle with paprika; arrange on serving platter. Garnish with lime wedges and preserved guava shells, if desired. Makes 4 servings.

CALIFORNIA SCALLOPS

¾ pound sea scallops
1 tablespoon salad oil
1 clove garlic, cut
2 medium tomatoes, halved
Salt
Pepper

1½ tablespoons lemon
   juice
1 tablespoon butter or
   margarine, melted
Lemon twists
Snipped parsley

About 50 minutes before serving:

1. Let scallops stand in salad oil with garlic for about 30 minutes.
2. Preheat broiler 10 minutes, or as manufacturer directs.
3. Meanwhile, sprinkle tomato halves with ½ teaspoon salt and ⅛ teaspoon pepper. In small shallow baking pan arrange tomato halves with scallops. Over scallops pour combined lemon juice, melted butter, ¼ teaspoon salt, and ⅛ teaspoon pepper.
4. Broil about 10 minutes, turning once.
5. Serve at once, with gravy spooned over scallops; garnish with lemon twists and parsley. Makes 2 servings.

CHINA SCALLOPS

1½ pounds fresh or
   thawed frozen sea
   scallops
1 medium cucumber
¼ cup butter or margarine
1 4-ounce jar pimentos,
   diced

1½ teaspoons salt
¼ cup catchup
1 cup milk
2 teaspoons cornstarch
2 tablespoons dry sherry
6 cups hot fluffy rice

1. Slice scallops crosswise into ¼-inch-thick disks. Pare cucumber; cut lengthwise into 16 strips, then crosswise into fourths.
2. In hot butter, in skillet, sauté scallops until golden —about 3 minutes. Add cucumber strips, pimentos, and salt; simmer, covered, 3 minutes. Add catchup and ½ cup milk.
3. Blend cornstarch with remaining ½ cup milk. Add to scallop mixture; cook, over medium heat, stirring, until boiling; stir in sherry.
4. Serve on hot fluffy rice. Makes 6 servings.

SCALLOPS EN BROCHETTE

½ cup packaged cracker
   meal
½ cup finely-crushed
   potato chips
1 teaspoon salt
1 teaspoon paprika
⅛ teaspoon pepper

2 pounds fresh or thawed
   frozen scallops
½ cup melted butter or
   margarine
6 lemon wedges
Bottled tartar sauce
   (optional)

About 45 minutes before serving:

1. Mix cracker meal with potato chips, salt, paprika, and pepper. Split any extra large scallops in half.
2. Dip scallops in melted butter, then coat each well with potato-chip mixture. Arrange scallops, about ½ inch apart, on 6 skewers.
3. Meanwhile, preheat broiler 10 minutes, or as manufacturer directs.
4. Line broiler pan with foil; lay skewers of scallops on broiler rack; sprinkle with rest of melted butter.
5. Broil 10 minutes, or until golden, turning occasionally.
6. Serve with lemon wedges and tartar sauce, if desired. Nice served with chilled tomato juice, frozen Brussels sprouts in butter sauce, instant mashed potatoes, piccalilli, and canned apricots. Makes 6 servings.

SHRIMP WITH GRAPES

¼ cup butter or margarine
¾ cup chopped celery
¼ cup chopped green
   pepper
¼ cup chopped onion
2 pounds raw shrimp,
   shelled, deveined

1 teaspoon salt
¼ teaspoon pepper
1 tablespoon bottled thick
   meat sauce
1 tablespoon lemon juice
1½ cups seedless green
   grapes

About 45 minutes before serving:

1. In large saucepan melt butter; in it sauté celery, green pepper, and onion until soft, stirring occasionally —about 10 minutes.
2. Add shrimp; sprinkle with salt and pepper; stir in meat sauce and lemon juice; then sauté until shrimp are pink. Now add grapes and cook 5 minutes longer. Nice served with hot fluffy rice, crisp tomato-cucumber salad, and brownies à la mode. Makes 6 servings.

SUPER SKILLET SHRIMP

2 cloves garlic, finely
   chopped
¼ cup salad oil
¼ cup butter or margarine
3 cups cooked shrimp (2½
   pounds raw)
½ teaspoon salt
⅛ teaspoon pepper
1 tablespoon regular all-
   purpose flour

½ cup dry white wine
½ teaspoon orégano
½ cup grated Parmesan
   cheese
4 teaspoons snipped parsley
½ cup fresh bread crumbs
About 3 cups hot fluffy
   rice

Day before:
Let garlic stand in oil, at room temperature, overnight; then remove garlic.

About 45 minutes before serving:

1. Start heating oven to 350°F.
2. In hot butter, in large skillet, heat shrimp; add salt and pepper. Spoon, without butter, into 1½-quart casserole or 4 individual casseroles.
3. Mix flour with a little wine; stir into butter in skillet. Simmer until light golden; stir in orégano, rest of wine, and garlic oil; pour all over shrimp. Combine Parmesan cheese, snipped parsley, and crumbs; sprinkle over shrimp.
4. Bake 30 minutes, or until light brown. Serve on hot rice. Makes 4 servings.

SHRIMP FLAMENCO

1 package herb- or Spanish-
   rice mix
1 package golden- or light-
   gravy mix
½ cup whole milk
½ cup undiluted evaporated
   milk

Dash cayenne pepper
Snipped parsley
2 8- to 10-ounce packages
   frozen, shelled, deveined
   shrimp

About 30 minutes before serving:

1. Cook rice as package label directs; keep warm.
2. Meanwhile, pour gravy mix into saucepan; stir in ½ cup water and whole milk until smooth. Bring to boil; simmer, stirring, 5 to 7 minutes, or until thickened. Stir in evaporated milk, cayenne, and 2 tablespoons snipped parsley; simmer 5 minutes.
3. In saucepan combine shrimp with enough water to cover; bring to boil, then simmer 3 minutes, or until all shrimp turn pink; drain.
4. Arrange shrimp in serving dish; pour sauce over them, then garnish with parsley. Serve with hot rice. Makes about 4 or 5 servings.

Pastas and Rice Dishes

SPAGHETTI AND CHEESE BALLS

Shortening or salad oil
 for deep-fat frying
½ pound spaghetti
1 can spaghetti sauce or
 1 package spaghetti-
 sauce mix
2 cups day-old bread
 crumbs, packed
¼ cup undiluted
 evaporated milk
¼ teaspoon salt

⅛ teaspoon nutmeg
2 eggs
1 8-ounce package shredded
 cheese food
1 tablespoon finely-snipped
 parsley
Packaged dried bread
 crumbs
¼ cup grated Parmesan
 cheese (optional)

About 1 hour before serving:
1. Start heating shortening in saucepan or electric skillet to 350°F. on deep-fat-frying thermometer, or until square of bread browns in 1 minute.
2. Meanwhile, prepare spaghetti and sauce as package labels direct.
3. Make Cheese Balls: Soak day-old bread crumbs in evaporated milk 5 minutes. Combine salt, nutmeg, and 1 egg, slightly beaten; add with shredded cheese and parsley to crumbs; mix well. Shape cheese mixture into about 14 1¼-inch balls. Roll balls in 1 slightly beaten egg, then in dried crumbs.
4. Fry Cheese Balls in hot shortening until golden—about 1 minute; drain on paper towels. Heap spaghetti on platter; top with sauce, cheese balls, then grated Parmesan. Makes 4 servings.

SPAGHETTI AND SHORT-RIB DINNER
(Pictured opposite)

7 beef short ribs (about
 5 pounds, untrimmed)
2 medium onions, sliced
2 teaspoons salt
½ teaspoon pepper
Granulated sugar
1 teaspoon whole allspice
4 bay leaves
2 beef-bouillon cubes

1 8-ounce package spaghetti
2 10-ounce packages frozen
 peas
1 15½-ounce can onions
Melted butter or margarine
Paprika
Grated Parmesan cheese
2 tablespoons regular all-
 purpose flour

About 2 hours and 30 minutes before serving:
1. Heat large Dutch oven until very hot. Add ribs, fat side down; cook over medium heat until well browned

—about 30 minutes. Lay sliced onions in fat around meat; cook a minute or so, or until browned. Add salt, pepper, 1 teaspoon sugar, allspice, bay leaves, bouillon cubes, and 2 cups hot water. Simmer, covered, 1½ to 2 hours, or until ribs are tender.
2. Meanwhile, cook spaghetti as package label directs. Cook peas as package label directs. Heat large, deep serving platter. In saucepan warm canned onions; toss in 2 tablespoons melted butter.
At serving time:
1. Drain spaghetti; heap in center of platter. Arrange short ribs around it, with peas and onions in between as pictured. Sprinkle with paprika. Sprinkle spaghetti with cheese, if desired.
2. Skim fat from liquid in Dutch oven. Slowly stir in ½ cup cold water blended with flour and 1 teaspoon sugar; cook until thickened; pass as gravy. Makes 7 servings.

SPAGHETTI ALLA ZINGARA

½ pound thin spaghetti
1 10-ounce package frozen
 tiny peas
Butter or margarine
½ pound fresh mushrooms,
 sliced

½ teaspoon salt
⅛ teaspoon pepper
¼ cup olive or salad oil
½ pound boiled ham, cut
 into thin strips
Grated Parmesan cheese

About 45 minutes before serving:
1. Cook spaghetti until tender as package label directs. Cook peas as package label directs; drain.
2. In medium skillet, heat 2 tablespoons butter; in it sauté mushrooms about 5 minutes; sprinkle with salt and pepper.
3. In large skillet, heat oil with 3 tablespoons butter; in it sauté ham lightly; add mushrooms and peas, then sauté 2 minutes. Now add 5 to 6 tablespoons hot water, then heat 2 minutes.
4. Drain spaghetti; arrange on large platter, pour on ham mixture; sprinkle with Parmesan cheese. Makes 4 to 6 servings.

CHEESE NOODLES WITH MEAT SAUCE

1 tablespoon shortening
1 small onion, chopped
1 pound chuck, ground
½ teaspoon salt
¼ teaspoon pepper

1 6-ounce package noodles
 with tomato-sauce mix
 and cheese
Boiling water
2 tablespoons butter or
 margarine
Snipped parsley

About 30 minutes before serving:
1. In hot shortening, in skillet, sauté onion and chuck until meat loses its red color. Then add salt, pepper, tomato-sauce mix, and 1⅓ cups boiling water; simmer, uncovered, about 10 minutes.

. Meanwhile, cook noodles as label directs; drain.
tir in butter, cheese mix, and ¼ cup boiling water.
. Arrange noodles in serving dish; pour on tomato-
eat sauce. Sprinkle with parsley. Makes 4 servings.

SKILLET MACARONI MEDLEY

¾ pound macaroni	2 8-ounce cans tomato
10-ounce package frozen	sauce
mixed vegetables	½ teaspoon salt
¼ cup butter or margarine	⅛ teaspoon pepper
onions, thinly sliced	

1. Cook macaroni as package label directs; drain.
2. Cook vegetables until tender, as package label di-
ects; drain.
3. Meanwhile, in hot butter, sauté onions until tender;
dd tomato sauce, salt, and pepper. Simmer 5 minutes.
Then fold in cooked macaroni and vegetables; heat.
Makes 6 servings.

RAVIETTI
(Pictured on page 19)

pound fresh pork-sausage	1 8-ounce package
links	Mozzarella cheese, sliced
2 15½-ounce cans beef	¼ teaspoon orégano
ravioli	3 tablespoons grated
15¾-ounce can meat	Parmesan cheese
balls in sauce	Snipped parsley (optional)

About 1 hour before serving:
1. Start heating oven to 425°F.

2. Arrange pork-sausage links in 10-by-6-by-2-inch
baking dish.
3. Bake 25 minutes, turning once; remove from baking
dish; pour off drippings.
4. In same baking dish arrange ravioli. Top with ½
can meat balls in sauce, half of sausages, then half of
cheese slices. Sprinkle with half of orégano. Repeat
layering and sprinkling, using rest of ingredients; then
sprinkle with Parmesan.
5. Bake 30 minutes, or until hot and bubbly. Sprinkle
with snipped parsley, if desired. Makes 4 servings.

RIO GRANDE RICE

2 tablespoons butter or	1 teaspoon paprika
margarine	1 6-ounce can tomato
6 frankfurters	paste
2 medium onions, chopped	1 10¾-ounce can con-
½ green pepper, chopped	densed consommé,
1 clove garlic, minced	undiluted
1 pound chuck, ground	2 cups hot cooked rice
1 teaspoon salt	1 cup drained cooked or
⅛ teaspoon pepper	canned peas
1 teaspoon chili powder	Grated Parmesan cheese

About 45 minutes before serving:
1. In large skillet, in hot butter, sauté frankfurters,
partially split lengthwise; remove, drain. In same skillet,
sauté onions, green pepper, garlic, and chuck, until meat
loses its red color; add salt, pepper, chili powder, paprika,
tomato paste, and consommé; cook 5 minutes, then stir
in cooked rice.

Spaghetti and Short Rib Dinner, Corned Beef, Virginia Style

3. Lightly grease 2-quart mixing bowl; around side stand up frankfurters, spoke-fashion, with cut side against bowl and one end meeting in center. Sprinkle a few peas in center bottom. Toss rest of peas with meat mixture.

4. Turn meat mixture into bowl; cover with foil and press down well so frankfurters are level with it. Invert a serving dish on top of bowl; quickly invert bowl and dish; lift off bowl. Sprinkle cheese down center of each frankfurter. Makes 6 servings.

CRAB-CHEESE PILAF

2 tablespoons salad oil	1 bay leaf, crumbled
1 cup chopped onion	1 tablespoon granulated
1 cup sliced celery	sugar
¼ cup diced green pepper	2 1-pound cans tomatoes
¼ pound sliced fresh	¾ cup packaged precooked
mushrooms, or 1 3- or 4-	rice
ounce can sliced mush-	2 6- to 7-ounce cans crab
rooms (optional)	meat
½ cup thinly-sliced	½ cup grated natural
carrots	Cheddar cheese
1 teaspoon salt	

1. Start heating oven to 350°F.

2. In hot salad oil, in large ovenproof skillet, sauté onion, celery, green pepper, mushrooms, and carrots until onion is golden-brown; add salt, bay leaf, sugar, and tomatoes; simmer 5 minutes. Stir in rice and crab meat; sprinkle cheese on top.

3. Bake 20 to 25 minutes. Serve in soup bowls, if desired. Makes 5 servings.

EAST-WEST STYLE CURRY OF EGGS

10 eggs	2 to 3 tablespoons curry
1 package seasoned-rice	powder
dish	2 tablespoons instant
4 cups packaged precooked	minced onion
white rice	1 soup can milk
1 10½-ounce can condensed	Salted peanuts
cream-of-mushroom	Seedless raisins
soup, undiluted	

*About 45 minutes before serving:**

1. Hard-cook eggs: Place eggs in pan, cover with warm water to cover tops by at least 1 inch. Cover; rapidly bring to boil. Turn heat very low and let stand, covered, 15 minutes. Cool thoroughly in cold water. Tap entire surface of egg to crackle shell; now roll between hands to loosen, then peel, starting at large end and dipping egg into bowl of cold water to ease off shell. Repeat.

2. Meanwhile, cook packaged seasoned-rice dish as label directs; season to taste; also cook precooked rice as label directs.

3. Make curry sauce: Place mushroom soup in sauce-pan; add curry powder and instant minced onion; st to blend. Gradually stir in milk. Simmer gently 5 mi utes, stirring occasionally.

4. Fix tray with small dishes of peanuts and raisin 4 hard-cooked eggs, halved, in medium bowl, and grav boat or pitcher of some of curry sauce.

At serving time:

1. Place all but 1 cup white rice on large serving dish heap seasoned-rice dish on top; then rest of white rice

2. Arrange 12 hard-cooked egg halves, cut side up around rice; spoon on a little curry sauce. Sprinkle few peanuts and raisins over top and sides.

3. In serving, spoon some of rice and a few eggs halve on each plate. Let each person top serving with addi tional egg halves, curry sauce, peanuts, and raisins from tray, as desired. Makes 6 to 8 servings.

*Eggs may be hard-cooked, shelled, and refrigerate ahead. Also the rice may be cooked ahead and kep warm for an hour or two.

GUEST HAMBURGER PILAF
(Pictured opposite)

3 tomatoes, each cut into	¼ cup butter or margarine
6 wedges	¼ cup chopped green
Salt	pepper
½ teaspoon pepper	½ cup chopped onion
Bottled French dressing	2 pounds chuck, ground
1 16-ounce package un-	2 teaspoons chili powder
cooked regular or	1 teaspoon monosodium
processed white rice	glutamate
2 cups cooked or canned	6 tablespoons catchup
peas	1 cup grated raw carrots
1 cup slivered toasted	Chutney
almonds	

About 40 minutes before serving:

1. Place tomato wedges in shallow dish; sprinkle with 2 teaspoons salt, and pepper. Then barely cover them with French dressing; set aside.

2. Cook rice as package label directs. Heat peas. When rice is done, combine with drained peas; toss lightly with toasted almonds, then with tomato wedges, drained; keep hot.

3. Meanwhile, in large skillet, in hot butter, sauté green pepper and onions until soft. With 2-tined fork, stir in chuck, 1 teaspoon salt, chili powder, and mono-sodium glutamate. Cook, stirring occasionally, until meat loses its red color. Then stir in catchup; simmer, uncovered, 10 to 15 minutes. Stir in raw carrots.

4. Lightly pile hot rice mixture in serving dish or platter; top with hamburger mixture. Then, if desired, spoon some chutney onto top center of hamburger mixture. Makes 10 to 12 servings.

FOR 5 OR 6: Halve all ingredients; make as directed above.

PAELLA VALENCIANA

⅓ cup salad oil
2 whole chicken breasts, split
4 chicken legs
1 cup chopped onion
1 clove garlic, minced
2 14-ounce cans chicken broth (4 cups)
1 teaspoon white pepper
3½ teaspoons salt
¾ teaspoon tarragon
½ teaspoon paprika
1 teaspoon saffron

2 cups uncooked regular white rice
1 16- or 17-ounce can tomatoes (2 cups)
3 chorizos (Spanish sausages), sliced*
1½ pounds shelled, deveined shrimp
12 littleneck clams or mussels
1 10-ounce package frozen peas
1 7-ounce can artichoke hearts

1. In salad oil, in Dutch oven, sauté chicken pieces until golden on all sides; remove chicken; set aside.
2. In same skillet, sauté onion and garlic until golden. Add chicken broth, pepper, salt, tarragon, paprika, and saffron; bring to boil. Add rice; cook, covered, over medium heat until about one-half liquid has been absorbed.
3. Now add tomatoes, chorizos, shrimp, and chicken; simmer, covered, about 30 minutes, or until rice is almost dry.
4. Meanwhile, steam clams in a little water until their shells pop open—about 10 minutes. Also, cook peas as package label directs.
5. Add peas and artichoke hearts to rice mixture; toss. Serve, heaped in 3-quart casserole or larger serving dish, with clams as garnish. Makes 8 servings.
*If not available, substitute pepperoni sausage, and add in step 3 toward end of 30 minutes.

Guest Hamburger Pilaf

Diet Dishes

DE LUXE PINEAPPLE MEAT LOAF
(low-calorie)

1 pound chuck, ground	1/4 cup minced onion
1 8-ounce can crushed pineapple, undrained	1/8 teaspoon prepared horse-radish
2 slices day-old bread, cubed	1 teaspoon salt
2 eggs	Catchup
	1/4 cup orange juice

1. Start heating oven to 350°F.
2. In 9-inch shallow baking pan mix together chuck, pineapple, bread cubes, eggs, onion, horse-radish, salt, and 2 tablespoons catchup until completely mixed. Gently form into long, narrow loaf about 9 by 5 by 2 inches. (Mixture will be soft.)
3. Bake 60 to 70 minutes, or to desired doneness.
4. While loaf is baking, prepare sauce: Stir together 2 tablespoons catchup and orange juice until smooth.
5. To serve, loosen loaf from bottom of pan; transfer to heated platter; cut into 12 slices. Pass sauce. Makes 6 servings of 2 slices each. (250 calories per serving)

LEMON-BARBECUED POT ROAST
(low-calorie)

1 3-pound sirloin tip	1/2 teaspoon celery salt
Seasoned instant meat tenderizer	1/2 teaspoon pepper
Water	1/4 teaspoon thyme
1/2 cup lemon juice	1 1/2 teaspoons cornstarch
2 cloves garlic, minced	1/2 teaspoon bottled sauce for gravy
1/4 cup minced onion	Lemon, thinly sliced
Salt	

Day before:
1. Treat meat with tenderizer as label directs. Place roast, fat side down, in small Dutch oven; heat to melt some of fat, then turn meat, as needed, to brown all sides. Add 2 cups water; simmer, covered, 1 hour. Cool, then cover and refrigerate overnight.
2. Meanwhile, in small jar, blend lemon juice with garlic, onion, 1/2 teaspoon salt, celery salt, pepper, and thyme. Refrigerate, covered, overnight.
About 3 hours before serving:
1. Remove roast from stock and trim off excess fat; skim fat from surface of stock. Strain lemon-garlic mixture; add liquid to stock in Dutch oven. Return meat to stock.

2. Simmer, covered, over low heat, about 2 hours and 30 minutes, or until meat is tender, adding water, if necessary. Remove meat from Dutch oven and cut, against grain, into 16 slices. Arrange slices on heated platter; keep hot.
3. Skim fat from stock; pour stock into measuring cup; add enough water to measure 1 cup; pour into Dutch oven. Stir in cornstarch until smooth; add bottled sauce for gravy. Heat, stirring constantly, until thickened; then add lemon slices and simmer a few minutes; add salt to taste. Pour some of this gravy over meat slices; pass rest. Makes 8 servings of 2 slices each. (310 calories per serving)

CHICKEN LIVERS IN WINE
(low-calorie)

1/2 pound chicken livers	1 large red cooking apple, cored, thinly sliced, then quartered (about 2 cups)
1 tablespoon butter or margarine	
1/4 cup thinly-sliced celery	1 teaspoon regular all-purpose flour
1/2 teaspoon dried minced parsley	Salt
1/2 teaspoon dried minced chives	Toast points prepared from 1 1/2 slices bread (optional)
2 whole cloves	
3/4 cup sherry	

1. Wash chicken livers; remove connective tissue. In hot butter, in medium skillet, sauté livers, celery, parsley, and chives until celery is light-brown.
2. Remove mixture from pan; add cloves, sherry and apples; simmer, covered, 5 minutes, or until apples are almost tender.
3. Make paste of flour and few drops water; stir into apple mixture; simmer until thickened. Return livers to pan; heat until warm; add salt to taste. Serve on toast points, if desired. Makes 3 servings. (170 calories per serving or 205 calories per serving if on toast)

OVEN-BAKED CHICKEN SUPREME
(low-calorie)

2 tablespoons melted butter or margarine	1/4 cup packaged dried bread crumbs
1/4 cup regular all-purpose flour	1/4 cup grated Parmesan cheese
1 teaspoon seasoned salt	2 large chicken breasts (about 1 pound), split, skinned, boned
1 egg, beaten	
1 tablespoon water	

1. Start heating oven to 350°F.
2. In 4 cereal bowls place melted butter and mixtures of flour and seasoned salt, beaten egg and water, and bread crumbs and cheese. Dip chicken pieces into butter, then lightly coat with seasoned flour. Then dip into

gg mixture and finally coat with crumb-cheese mixture.

Fit a rack into 9-inch shallow baking dish; arrange reasts close together on rack.

. Bake 45 minutes, or until chicken is fork-tender, ut still juicy. Do not overcook.

. Remove chicken from oven; then preheat broiler 0 minutes, or as manufacturer directs. Run baking dish nder broiler a few minutes to lightly brown crust; then erve immediately. Makes 4 servings. *(250 calories per erving)*

CHICKEN-VEGETABLE PILAF
(low-calorie, low-fat)

¼ cup regular all-purpose flour
easoned salt
whole chicken breasts, split, skinned, boned, and cut into bite-size pieces (about 2 pounds)
tablespoons butter or margarine
cups water
cup uncooked regular long-grain rice
teaspoon salt
⅛ teaspoon pepper
1 medium onion, chopped, or 2 tablespoons instant minced onion
2 stalks green celery, thinly sliced
2 chicken-bouillon cubes or envelopes chicken-broth mix
1 10-ounce package frozen Italian green beans
2 medium tomatoes, cut into eighths

About 45 minutes before serving:

. Mix together flour and 1 teaspoon seasoned salt; use to coat chicken cubes evenly. In hot butter, in very large skillet, with tight-fitting lid, sauté chicken until lightly browned.

. Add water, rice, salt, pepper, onion, celery, and bouillon cubes; bring to simmer and stir thoroughly.

. Place frozen beans on top of simmering mixture. Lay tomato wedges around edge of skillet; generously sprinkle tomato wedges and beans with seasoned salt. Simmer, covered, 15 minutes (separate beans with fork after 5 minutes), or until beans are tender-crisp, but still bright green. Serve immediately. Makes 6 servings. *(320 calories per serving and 5 grams fat)*

BAKED SWORDFISH AU GRATIN
(low-calorie)

1 pound fresh or thawed frozen swordfish steaks, ½ to ¾ inch thick
½ cup salad oil
½ cup sauterne
1 teaspoon dried parsley flakes
¼ teaspoon thyme
1 bay leaf, crumbled
6 whole peppercorns
1 small onion, thinly sliced
⅓ cup packaged dried bread crumbs
⅓ cup grated Parmesan cheese
¼ teaspoon orégano
½ teaspoon salt

1. Cut swordfish steaks into 4 portions. In shallow baking pan combine salad oil, sauterne, parsley, thyme, bay leaf, peppercorns, and onion; lay swordfish on top; refrigerate at least 2 hours, occasionally spooning marinade over fish.
2. Start heating oven to 350°F.
3. Combine bread crumbs, cheese, orégano, and salt; use to coat fish steaks. Lay steaks in shallow baking dish.
4. Bake, covered, 20 minutes; then uncover and bake 15 minutes longer, or until fish flakes, but is still moist. If browner surface is desired, run under broiler until light-brown. Makes 4 servings. *(210 calories per serving)*

SHRIMP, SAILOR STYLE
(low-calorie, low-fat)

1 1-pound 1-ounce can Italian tomatoes, undrained
2 tablespoons finely-snipped parsley
2 cups sliced celery
¼ teaspoon basil
1½ teaspoons seasoned salt
⅛ teaspoon pepper
½ teaspoon orégano
½ 6-ounce can tomato paste
2 cups water
1 teaspoon salt
1 cup uncooked regular long-grain rice
2 7-ounce packages frozen, shelled, deveined shrimp

About 45 to 50 minutes before serving:

1. In large skillet or Dutch oven mix together undrained tomatoes, parsley, celery, basil, seasoned salt, pepper, orégano, and tomato paste. Simmer gently, stirring occasionally, uncovered, 30 minutes, or until celery is almost tender.
2. Meanwhile, in medium saucepan, bring water to simmer; add salt, then rice. Bring mixture to simmer, stir once or twice, turn down heat, cover, then simmer gently about 15 minutes, or until liquid is absorbed and rice is tender. Turn off heat, fluff up rice with fork, cover, and let stand on burner until serving.
3. Stir frozen shrimp into tomato sauce. Simmer gently 5 to 10 minutes, or until shrimp are cooked and tender. Serve over rice—about ⅔ cup rice and ¾ cup sauce per serving. Makes 5 servings. *(285 calories per serving, negligible fat)*

Index

IMPORTANT ANNOUNCEMENT FOR PARENTS OF YOUNG CHILDREN

A GREAT
LEARNING & FUN PACKAGE

WORTH $13^{15}

YOURS FOR ONLY $1^{00}

See Next Page →

IMPORTANT ANNOUNCEMENT FOR PARENTS OF YOUNG CHILDREN!

ABSOLUTELY FREE *for your child!*

THE NEW COLOR-PICTURE DICTIONARY FOR CHILDREN

★ over 1500 words defined from New Webster's Dictionary!

★ more than 800 pictures in full color!

★ a full 8⅝" x 11" —a $6.95 retail value!

ABSOLUTELY FREE *for your child with trial enrollment in*

The Treasure House

Big Book Club

At last! Yes...thousands of mothers and fathers across the nation are saying: "At last! A book program for my child that gets away from the small, over-priced, quick-to-read, quick-to-throw-away books."

And that is truly the purpose of The Treasure House BIG BOOK Club: to offer the best in children's literature and learning materials...either in oversized, giant book format or in multi-volume sets...for the lasting enjoyment of children. And equally important, at significant sayings!

Under The Guidance Of An Outstanding Panel of Educators And Reading Specialists

Each selection of The Treasure House BIG BOOK Club is thoroughly scrutinized and examined by an expert panel of children's educators and reading specialists. They select only books of outstanding literary and learning value...books that encourage and stimulate the child to read and read and read—books so substantial that they will be passed on from child to child in the family, never losing their fascination, and eventually becoming...

A Permanent Part of the Family's Library!

For these will be books and stories by such all time greats as Charles Dickens, Rudyard Kipling, Hans Christian Andersen, Robert Louis Stevenson and many others, as well as by such present-day favorites as Walt Disney, Richard Scarry, Charles Schulz, Hilda Boswell, Kate Greenaway and a great host of others.

A New BIG BOOK Every Six Weeks At a Big 20% to 40% Savings To You—Plus A Fascinating Newsletter!

Unlike other children's book clubs and programs which usually ship a small book every month, The Treasure House BIG BOOK Club will ship your child a new book *every six weeks*. The reason is simple: Our selections are big and substantial—it takes a child longer to examine, read, and savor them. Each selection comes to you at a savings ranging from a minimum of 20% to a great big 40%! But, that's not all! You and your child will also receive...free...a colorful, informative newsletter filled with news about children's books, important guidance tips from reading specialists, plus previews of books to come!

Your Child's First Selection (a $3.95 value) —Yours for Only $1 With Trial Enrollment!

Your child's first selection, TREASURY OF CHILDREN'S STORIES, is a clear indication of the kind of book your child will receive every six weeks as a member—a big 8⅜" x 10¾" volume of 128 pages, illustrated in full color—an anthology of stories personally selected and beautifully illustrated by Hilda Boswell...including works of such famous authors as C.S. Lewis, Charles Dickens, Hans Christian Andersen, Oscar Wilde, and others! Truly one of the most beautiful anthologies ever published!

Also FREE,
for you, if you act within 10 days!
THE NEW WEBSTER'S DICTIONARY, Vest Pocket Edition

To encourage you, the parent, to enroll **your child now**...and give him the pleasure of membership as rapidly as possible—we'll also send, absolutely free, the newly published Vest Pocket Edition of Webster's Dictionary. This small but handy reference volume is free to keep even if you decide not to continue your child as a member!

ALL THIS—your child's first selection, "Treasury of Children's Stories," plus the two free dictionaries—A Great Book Package Worth $13.15—Is Yours For Only $1! So, with nothing to lose and so much to gain...enroll your child today!

Use Envelope On Next Page →

TO ENROLL—1. FILL IN COUPON ON REVERSE SIDE
(DO NOT TEAR COUPON FROM PAGE).

2. CAREFULLY DETACH THIS ENTIRE PAGE FROM BOOK
AND FOLD AS INSTRUCTED BELOW.

3. ENCLOSE YOUR DOLLAR REMITTANCE.

4. SEAL, STAMP, AND MAIL.

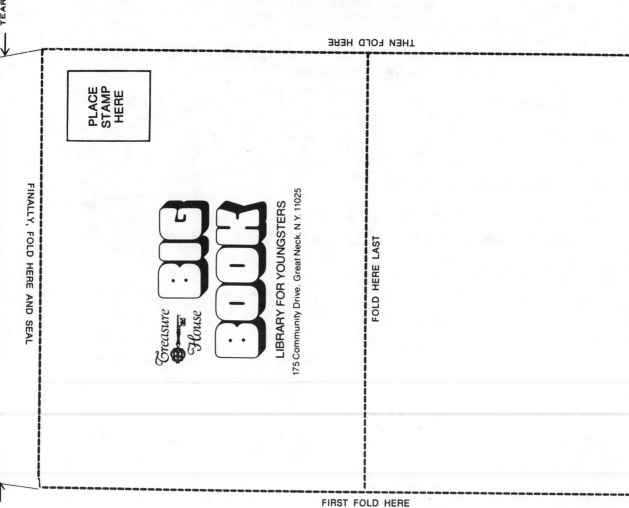

TEAR ALONG PERFORATION TO MAKE FLAP

THEN FOLD HERE

PLACE STAMP HERE

FINALLY, FOLD HERE AND SEAL

Treasure House **BIG BOOK**

LIBRARY FOR YOUNGSTERS

175 Community Drive, Great Neck, N.Y. 11025

FOLD HERE LAST

DETACH CAREFULLY BEFORE FOLDING TO MAIL

TEAR ALONG PERFORATION TO MAKE FLAP

FIRST FOLD HERE